Who You Choose to Be

By Carrie Spratley

Published by Heather Andrews

Follow It Thru Publishing

www.followitthrupublishing.com

www.heatherandrews.press

ISBN: 978-1-5136-4746-3

Table of Contents

Foreword

I would be remiss if I didn't take the time to publicly express my gratitude. Gratitude takes us to a place where we choose to see what is good, no matter what our circumstances may be. It's a choice we make, and it is powerful one. I choose gratitude.

I would not be who I am, or where I am, at without my amazing savior, Jesus Christ, who has drawn me closer to Him with each passing day. None of this is possible without Him.

To my devoted, faithful, loving, supportive, head cheerleader Eric, my best friend: I am who I am because of who we are together. It is by design and it is a beautiful blend of God's faithfulness, grace, and endless mercy.

My amazing gifts, the three young men God has given me the blessing to raise. I could not be prouder of each of you at this very moment. I am who I am, because you made me want to be the best I could be for you.

My friends, who are also by design, who have loved me, prayed for me, and cheered me on over the years: you KNOW who you are. You too have had a huge hand in inspiring me to live a life that matters and how important our choices are. I choose you!

My parents, who have given me all the love, support and prayers over the years, and ultimately set the foundation I have on solid ground with a saving faith in Jesus. For that I will always be grateful.

My family who has also given me the permission to be who God created me to be: thank you for being the support system I need to make God famous on this side of eternity.

To my church family: every single one of you, thank you for being there for me and for showing me who Jesus is, as you love me and others like Jesus. Pastor Dan, thank you for your words of wisdom you share each and every week. I would not have grown to the capacity I have without your wise counsel. To my small group: thank you for pouring into my life in such unique and profound ways. I love each of you.

To my friend who introduced me to some amazing supplements that were a game changer for my healing: thank you for that fateful text message that has not only changed my life, but the lives of so many others.

To my amazing photographer who I shared a vision with and who ran with it: you are a blessing and I am grateful that God gave me you.

To my friend who introduced me to my publisher: thank you for choosing to have impact through me by linking my arms with a company who would help get my message out to the world.

To my publishing team: what a wild ride this has been! I am so grateful for all of the learning curves and grace given to one another in this process. Thank you for moving all the mountains you did and for believing in me.

Chapter 1: The Gift of Being Present

Time is an unknown variable in the equation of life: it's safe to say that what time we have is borrowed. Time doesn't actually belong to us, yet we use it like we own it and that this resource is unending. We take it for granted and we spend it flippantly. We should make the most of our time, since we've no idea how much of it we're allotted, but perhaps that's becoming increasingly difficult to do. We try to carve out time for the things that matter most to us, but I've realized that all too often, we can be physically present in life but not really here at all.

Earlier this summer my husband and I were reading a book together, which was helping us dialog some questions relating to our marriage and how certain behaviors can cause us to be less 'present' than we would like. Even though we are physically present, that doesn't mean our attention or intentions are fully *here.*

For instance, my husband Eric and I were meeting up during the day, cell phones close at hand, talking about various things happening in our day when I received a text. Eric continued to talk, and I was still "listening," nodding at him while I viewed the text message and responded to the message. We continued to "converse" back and forth. At the end of our "conversation" he politely asked me to repeat what he had just said.

This kind of communication grieves my soul. We attempt to communicate and walk away feeling we failed to truly connect and be *present*. Even though questions get answered and "listening" takes place, we walk away feeling unheard, not validated, or misunderstood.

That's just one example, but there are many more and it happens both ways. My husband and I have reflected on those experiences many times, discussing how we both have had times when life goes flying by—our plates overflowing, topped off with a side of low carb chaos. It's in those times we find ourselves having "conversations" with one another that are distracted at best. We are so busy looking at a text from one person while fielding an in person "conversation" with another, that we have to admit we aren't giving any one person the careful consideration they deserve. Does this sound familiar?

When did we all decide to become these master jugglers, thinking that it was okay or even effective to fill our plates with all of these activities simultaneously, crunch them together, and call it a "life?" We've harnessed the power of all of this technology, allegedly designed to save us time and help us better communicate and connect, yet we feel more divided, stressed, and disconnected than ever before. We believe we are communicating, and others respond, yet we often walk away not feeling heard or understood. And does it even matter, as time charges forward regardless of the misunderstandings, half-attention, and missed cues we send to one another?

We do this with our time *a lot*. We are present, but not *actually* here.

Intention

After having this powerful dialog, Eric and I decided our relationship was worth being more intentional with one another, including having undivided conversations with each other. We made sure that when we were soliciting each other's time for conversation, that it was a good time to go over something, rather than just *presuming* it was a good time.

I cannot emphasize enough how important it is that we not miss opportunities to truly connect with each other. Our time in this life is limited, and where we put our attention matters more than we might think. Taking the time to gather more information from the One who made us is critically important as we forge ahead in our businesses, too. What it is that He desires we do on this side of eternity? What will actually hold its value, and when we "resell" this body in for the new one, has its value increased?

Prior to becoming a holistic health coach, I was a real estate agent for about 10 years. Some years, my efforts in this field were more fruitful than others as I battled an autoimmune illness that made success a challenging prospect at times. One of the reasons I got into real estate was that I liked to help people, and I always had an eye on the "condition" of the different areas where we lived. I was always paying attention and keenly aware of what the neighborhood looked like. Was it becoming run down, was it showing signs of improvement, or was the area sustaining its value?

We didn't have a lot of financial investments, so our home was always our largest asset. I cared about whether or not we were gaining or losing value. I was able to discern when things were starting to decline and would make suggestions that it might be a good time to reinvest our equity in the next up-and-coming area to increase the return on our investment. Our lives are a lot like this in a way. We were designed to add value to others and to gain value as we grow and develop. Even life's challenges, produce gain. It's important for us to perceive it in a valuable manner.

We are here to add value to others' lives and in that process, we gain value in our asset. We become a better and better asset with each challenge we face and overcome. We refine. We mature. When we choose to be present for others in the depths of their pain, we add value to the depth of what we are able give. *When we go through hardship, we are actually increasing the value of what we have to offer this world*. The setbacks we experience all have purpose for the greater good. The Bible says to consider it a joy when we experience a trial. *Its adding value to our own lives so that we, in turn, can add value to the lives of others*. It's what we do with the asset of life that appears as though it has a negative dividend when in all actuality it's gaining tremendous value for eternity.

Identity and Purpose

Who am I? And, why does who I am matter? Perhaps the more we know, the more we can be held accountable for. Thank you for your careful consideration of spending your hard-earned resources on this offering of a book that God unexpectedly placed words for in my path on this side of eternity. My name is Carrie and I am humbled to share with you some pieces of wisdom from my heart to yours.

I come to you from the beautiful area of Northern Nevada, about 30 minutes from Lake Tahoe, California. I am married to my best friend who is a retired lieutenant from our local sheriff's office. We have raised three young men who we treasure and are so proud of. I absolutely cannot believe how fast time flew by from the day they were born. God blessed us with one amazing daughter-in-law, married to our oldest son, and we could not be more grateful for the family that she came with. Running around our home are two of the most spoiled female Boston Terriers you will ever encounter, who fill a space in our hearts we cannot fathom being empty. We spend most of our days serving people in our local community and with those we love the most. I am a board Certified Holistic Health Coach and absolutely love the opportunity to work with people locally and abroad.

God brought me out of a place of survival to a place where I thrive. Through that process, I promised Him that as long as there were people who needed help in areas I knew I could help, I would share my story of hope with them. I am grateful to have been given the gift of healing and believe that God created space and time in my life to heal. It felt tragic at the time, but deep down I knew I was fighting for a greater purpose. In the scheme of it all, we have had some amazing experiences in this life, having been afforded opportunities most people would only dream of, to which many have failed to fill that space in our soul we thought would be valuable. So, we have sought wise counsel for living more of a life that matters most on this side of eternity.

My hope is that as I share both the difficult and the profound life lessons we have experienced, that you can find a place in your heart to consider what it is God has allowed in your life that could be used *with purpose, for a purpose, and on purpose that matters most.* I believe we all have choices in how we respond to life's challenges, and in the end what **we choose** truly does matter.

Recently I was going through some pictures of us sifting through the debris of fire ravaged homes as part of the Paradise, California disaster relief effort. Something profound resonated with me as I looked at these photos. **It's not about what we find, it's who we choose to be**. We all have choices about how we spend our time, our money, our talents and abilities, and to determine our intention in the moments that matter.

When we believe that what each of us has to offer other people on this side of eternity has great value, and that how we ration those offerings out to others really does matter—it is an amazing opportunity for life's true purpose to unfold. It isn't always about what we have to offer, but more about who is doing the offering. It's important that we choose to be present, aware, intentional, and purposeful with each moment that is gifted to us by God. We need to steward our time like it's the last $100 we have. If we know that $100 is all we have access to, we can be acutely aware of how and where we spend it. What we don't know is how much time each of us have been given.

A friend recently commented on our disaster relief efforts, saying it must be neat to help people find their valuables when sorting through what was left of their home. That made me think, because we've never actually recovered anything of significant monetary value, nor have we seen other people recover such items. It's the *act* of searching, of helping, and of showing up for others when there is no motive otherwise. And that is what equates to eternal value.

Our reward is the blessing on our lives when we say "yes" to being there in other people's pain. And when I say "blessing" I don't mean something physically or monetarily. The "blessing" is the space in your soul that becomes more complete when we make a way to be present for others. The look on people's faces when a group of twenty-five strangers from all over the country shows up to be with them in the depths of their sadness is worth the commodity of time spent.

Feel Felt Found

Feel/Felt/Found is a concept that brings validation to an experience. For example, if I share with someone that I have had a miscarriage and that person has never had a miscarriage, they don't know how I feel since they haven't experienced it. However, when I share that information with someone who has, they know how I feel. Sometimes we are given the holy responsibility to go through a difficult time, a tragedy, losses of varying degrees simply so we can validate others experiences, and show them there *is* hope for survival. When someone's home burns down and another person whose home also burned down can show up, be present, and encourage them that recovery is possible—*this* is the real treasure to be found in the situation.

We go through hard circumstances and in many instances, it is to show others recovery is possible. When that hard assignment comes our way, we are to receive it as a gift. *Sometimes it may seem like the dreaded white elephant gift, but even those can be a real treasure!* We can *choose* to validate other human beings in their pain by saying, I know how you feel, I have felt the same way, and here is what I found that helped me get through a similar situation. It's a powerful gesture to say yes to tragedy in our own lives. *When we accept the reality that the world doesn't revolve around us and that we aren't put here to be self-focused and self-gratifying, but focus on what it is our own experiences can offer other people, our lives will take a powerful trajectory in the pursuit of making an intentional impact, by being present for others. It is the best gift we can give.*

Last Sunday while cleaning up from serving coffee at our church, I ran into a sweet friend. She asked me about a recent trip Eric and I made to California to help with a disaster relief effort through an organization called Samaritan's' Purse. While sharing stories back and forth about the summer, I reached into the cupboard to get my purse. When I lifted it up, it quickly dawned on me that my purse was filthy. I was so embarrassed! Then remembered why my purse was so dirty.

It was dirty with the soot of other people's lives. It was dirty because I chose to be part of a movement to help others rise from their ashes. That purse sat on the floor of a dirty truck and dirty driveways of the people who had suffered great losses in the California fires. I was comforted in that moment, knowing that God restores the brokenhearted and uses ordinary people like me to be there for others in dire circumstances. That dirty purse had been with me and was evidence of our intentional decision to step out in faith and obedience to a calling that really mattered.

There was no need for me to be embarrassed about the evidence of that experience, as God had used us to be there for others in their time of need. It seems selfish to experience things of such gravity and not share how impactful they are and how important it is that we show up in other people's lives, with the clear intent of just being there to help. We are often so unfocused and hurried to get on to whatever's next on our agenda, that we don't slow down long enough to have conversations that matter. I wanted my friend to know that what we did, she could do, that *anyone* could do. And that even though it was physically and emotionally one of the hardest weeks of my life, it was also one of the most fulfilling, an experience that has filled a space in our hearts we didn't know existed; and not only us, but for those who we were there to help.

Speak It

Further into our conversation, I found myself looking for words that would truly capture our experience, to share it with her in a way that she would understand the magnitude of it. I found myself looking to inspire her in a way that she or anyone else could understand that God can use ANYONE as a tool to help others. Then something crazy happened: I spoke the words out loud.

"You want to hear something weird? I think I am supposed to write a book about this," I said in a conspiratorial tone. This was the third time I spoke those same eight words out loud. As the words left my mouth, I thought to myself, *Why do I keep saying that?*

My initial reaction was that I wanted to take my hand, cover my mouth, and excuse myself for using inappropriate language. I am not one to say things of that significance so flippantly if I don't actually *mean* them, or given thought and prayer to them first. I first spoke these words aloud to Eric, about two weeks before, on our way home from helping with the fires. Then a week later, I was walking with Charlene, my son's mother-in-law and out it came again.

Each time I said these words, it felt somehow ordained, as though God had planted it on my heart; something I needed to be accountable for and share with the world.

What was I getting myself into by making such a statement? Would I be "that girl" who walks around telling people she is going to write a book and not have a single clue what that looks like, or have the slightest idea of what to say, or better yet, the actual ability to do it? I had never even considered myself to be worthy of having the ability to write a book. It has always been my perception that people who write books are super smart and have it all together—not something I ever considered myself to be. When I started school in the mid '70s, I have profound memories of struggling with concepts that most of my peers were connecting the dots with.

It was later in life that I realized I was very young for my grade, having a fall birthday. I started kindergarten when I was four and turned five after the first part of that year. When you have twelve years of education never feeling like you were grasping concepts as well as the other kids, considering myself intelligent enough to ever have the capacity to write a book was not on my radar. What I have since learned is that it doesn't matter what we consider ourselves to be capable of doing, as we shouldn't be operating out of our own strengths regarding things that matter. God equips those He calls to do His work, and we simply move the hands, the feet, and the keystrokes on a keyboard. His intention is mightier than any ability I might think I have or not.

Do It

With each passing day after making this bold statement to people that matter, I was feeling more and more called to actually put pen to paper. It was one of those things that was just *happening,* and I didn't know how, what, or why. *Was it a sure thing? Would it be a waste of my time?* I consider myself to be somewhat calculated with decision-making and activities generally need to make sense in my mind as I process logistics and practicality. However, each of the three times I spoke these words about feeling called to write a book, the resounding response from each person was the same, "DO IT!" *Was that a coincidence? For all three people to have the same response? Do I just have the biggest cheerleaders in my life that say what I want to hear? Did I subconsciously share it with people who I KNEW would encourage me?*

I was feeling empowered, yet somehow had no idea really what to say exactly or do. I just knew that I felt like there were experiences and lessons, good and bad, all coming to a head. As a result, I felt compelled for people to know what those things were, and in doing so, may create a positive ripple effect that would help other people see who they were created to become. I wanted readers to see what God can do through their lives when they too, step into the unknown and ask God to use them to demonstrate His love.

I have read many books in my forty-six years of life. Never once in those times did I ever see myself being an author of something another person would want to read. Nor did I ever consider myself to be the caliber of writer to write a book others would read. I enjoyed writing and have written a few blogs, but never in my wildest dreams did I ever consider a book! It's amazing what we open ourselves up to when we follow unforeseen and unexpected ways God can use us as we step out in faith and in confidence that we are His vessels. When He is with us, unique and profound things can and will unfold when we say yes to the calls He puts on our hearts and sends us the encouragement we need.

Just this morning, I was pondering in my quiet time with God. It became more and more obvious that I was to at least *start* doing something. The method to this potential madness was unclear, yet the pains of birth were becoming so evident that this baby was not going back in the womb. It was almost as if the words started to pour out, like floodgates opening, with what God had placed in my heart to share. There have been so many times in my life that I have been given clarity and hope from books I have read. I wondered, *is this what those authors felt?* I frantically began looking for paper to start writing, then I quickly realized, *Carrie, if this is really happening, you type considerably faster than you write.*

I scrambled for the laptop as if the words were like water, spilling from my glass, encouraging me to keep pouring, and didn't want it to hit the ground, so I started typing.

Chapter 2: Words that Matter

There is power in our words. They are either life-breathing or life-taking. They say for every negative word spoken, it takes ten positives to neutralize that *one* negative.

What other people speak over us is equally, if not more, powerful than what we think of ourselves, as we often crave validation, worrying about what others see us as. We become paralyzed in our potential when we give thought to how we are being perceived. I learned a few years ago when I read a book by Bruce Wilkinson that God, the creator of the universe, puts desires in each of our hearts, specifically dreams, for a reason and bigger purpose far beyond our wildest imaginations. After reading the first few chapters of the book on my own and seeing how I was immediately impacted by what I was reading, I decided it would be an even better read with Eric and my youngest son Caleb, as he was our last son still living at home. The allegorical book, *The Dream Giver*, talks about how God is the giver of our dreams, and how it's important to learn and identify what dreams He has given each of us.

As we read one chapter per night, we began to talk to each other about what God had put in each of our hearts. If you ever find yourself learning something new and you immediately think of people that could be impacted by what you are reading or learning, please share it with them. I found it to be extremely helpful to learn and know what my husband and son's dreams were. It also taught me to edify and encourage those dreams and not be the one who kills another's dream. I am their biggest cheerleader when it comes to working out the desires God places in their hearts.

There is power we can bring to these dreams God gives us when we speak them out loud. Have you ever purchased a new car and once you have the new car, you suddenly see that particular kind of car everywhere? There is some science to that. We have a mechanism at the back of our brains that is called our reticular activating system. When we log things in and validate them as things of value, they are what we will notice. We truly bring about what we think about. Not only is this an important part of a journey to do more of what matters, it's important that those around you know too. They can encourage, support and, in my case, help make it happen.

As a society, our dreams are not something we talk much about, because they seem so far off in the future or farfetched. They often feel unattainable and fantasy-like. Why would God give us desires that were fantasy? Doesn't it seem more validating that He would give us desires that could be impactful, purposeful, and attainable? After all, if God is for us in the desires He puts in our hearts, who can be against us? Plenty, I tell you! There are PLENTY of people who don't want us to see our dreams unfold. Most people don't believe their dreams are even *possible. Inmates don't like to see other inmates escape.* It's important that we surround ourselves with doers, thinkers, and fellow dreamers. These are OUR people. I want the people I surround myself with to be my biggest cheerleaders and you should too. Be the person who cheers people on and encourages them regardless of how farfetched it may seem. Who are we to say what can and cannot be done? *When God gives us a yes that is what matters the most.* After all, they aren't the ones that created us with purpose, for purpose, and on purpose. Why would we give credence to their truth about us?

I remember overhearing someone that I would consider to be a dear friend talk about my decision to go to nutrition school and said that she didn't think it was necessary for me to pursue that. I found it strange that someone would have such an unfair judgment about my life. I hadn't made a decision to pursue illegal activity or something that would go against my faith. It would seem as though making the decision to further my education would be something that a friend would validate, cheer on, and encourage. I can only imagine what the reasoning would be since it didn't make sense. Then I realized that this opinion of me didn't matter. Once I released that opinion, I felt free to pursue with confidence the call to enter into my education in nutrition. Typically, it's safe to say that when people have those kinds of perceptions about truth for our lives, it is generally a reflection of their hearts. **Bless and release those who don't always have clarity about who they are to understand who you are.**

When I was in the throes of early marriage and motherhood—which eventfully collided at the same time—I learned some incredible lessons. I still continue to learn a lot of life lessons as a result of our choices, even back then. To say I was moved on many levels, being the age I was and at the speed with which it was unfolding, was nothing short of a miracle. When I look back now, it is obvious that, statistically, we should have failed. We had two boys close together, only twenty months apart. Their names are Jared and Garrett. Fortunately for me, being so young, not a whole lot bothered or stressed me out. I simply didn't know any better. While I realize that having one in diapers, not quite walking yet, and cutting his first tooth seemed like a logical choice for timing to have another, we clearly had no idea what it meant to have two kids under the age of two.

Anything but the Kids

Jared and Garrett are very different. Jared is the oldest, most calculating and cautious one. Garrett is adventurous, marches to the beat of his own drum, and takes risks. I would often share a word picture story with people when referring to the difference as if they were both perched on the top bunk of their bunk bed:

while one was negotiating the odds and math of what would happen if they jumped off, the other was in the air doing it. Jared was the thinker and Garrett was the jumper. Time escaped us every year and I found myself pacing through life with a new marriage and two boys who made all in my world right. They gave me a run for my money on many days, but I loved every moment, despite my young age. I look back now and wonder who that girl was, embracing marriage and motherhood as I did. I love my boys deeply. I have always "negotiated" with God. I would say "anything but the kids" or "you can have anything, but the kids are off limits." Be careful what you tell God you are not capable of doing.

When my friends were graduating high school and going onto college, I felt like I was on an island of misfits, as I didn't have a desire to go to college or be someone fancy. I didn't have these grandiose plans for a career or felt any calling in any specific direction of any given field. I even tried going to college and felt like I didn't belong and was not supposed to be there. I had a deep profound calling to be a mom. I know we are all different and that many women out there desire a career and family, and they find great joy with both. I desperately desired to be the mom that was present as often as possible. I was so grateful that I was even given the opportunity to be a mom, as I know so many women ache for motherhood, but they cannot. In fact, after having Jared and Garrett and thinking two boys for our family was sufficient, I often gave a lot of thought to being a surrogate mom so that I could help someone have a baby who otherwise could not. Grateful for what I had, I soaked motherhood in and cherished the days.

Grandpa Veryl

Back in the '90s, we did not have social media like we do today. We didn't have this virtual minute-by-minute opportunity to update our "story" or a newsfeed status for all the days and moments of our lives. So, every year at Christmastime I would write a family letter that went hand in hand with our dutifully picture-perfect Christmas card. We actually took said picture on a *camera* that had *film*. We would take that film to a local developer, sort through what was the best, and have it developed. Typically, this took a few days and when we got really fancy as times progressed, we could have it overnight or better yet, in an hour! In this letter, I recounted the highlights of our year on paper and pass it out to those nearest and dearest to us. I would share about our travels, activities, and adventures in one page or less.

My grandfather, on my mom's side, is one of my heroes. He was what I refer to as a quiet giant, standing over six feet tall. He was introverted, yet when he spoke, he commanded our attention. He loved to tell stories. He was always great at communicating what was happening in others' lives in a way that you felt like you were there. He always had a pack of Doublemint gum in his shirt pocket and loved to eat homemade popcorn popped from a pressure cooker, cooked with Crisco oil while playing card games. His smile was something special and I treasured every single one I saw. His words were precious, a melody to my ears. You knew if he was speaking, they were wise words. He was prudent with his money. He was not terribly affectionate, but he showed us love by doing things with us, like taking us to the Rose Parade or a Dodgers baseball game. He was a wonderful grandfather. I have mounds of memories that I will always treasure about my Grandpa Veryl. Grandma Mary, was also a treasure: she was an amazing cook and loved us in unique ways. They lived in California, about 7 hours from where we spent most of our youth. When we were really young, we lived closer to them. We would stay overnight at their house on a Saturday and Grandma Mary would bribe us with a cinnamon twist doughnut on a Sunday morning if we went to church with her. I can still smell the frosting and the cinnamon to this day.

Family mattered to my grandparents. Every few years we would all gather for a family reunion at different destinations throughout the states where my parents, their siblings, cousins, and kids would all meet for a week at a time. We would camp and play cards and sit around a campfire. So many treasured memories were made with my aunts, uncles, grandparents, and cousins. One year, we were sitting around the table playing cards and eating popcorn when my grandfather began sharing something with me that I now see as profound and ordained. He discussed with me how much he valued getting my Christmas letter and card. He said I had a way with words and that I made him laugh. He said I shared our year in highlights in a way that was meaningful, and he said I had a gift to write. Words are powerful. The earth may have stopped spinning on its axis for a moment as I soaked in what those words meant to me. Even recounting this memory brings tears to my eyes. *He spoke life into me with those words.*

Why in the world would these words resonate with me so much? Why would I remember them years later, when I felt God tugging on my heart to put pen to paper and write what I feel compelled to share? He mattered to me. What he thought of me mattered. What he shared with me that day—I have not thought about for years, but it certainly matters today, as his words breathe life and power pours into my being. Little did he know, words he spoke long ago would one day lead to another layer of confidence in an area of my life. God was calling me to do it, to write. While the confidence to do what we feel called to do helps, it's not needed. We simply need the yes from God and the faith to believe He is our sole source of strength, inspiration. In that faith is all the confidence we need.

One would think that if you set out to do something "good" that everything will come together effortlessly, right? You better believe the fierce reality that when we step out in faith, boldness and move on what God calls us to do, the enemy will be the biggest naysayer, whispering words of doubt: "you can't do this," or "no one will want to hear what you have to say." Layers upon layers of opposition from the enemy will try to thwart God's plan on every level. Surely, the enemy knows how BIG and how powerful my God is! We can release any fear or doubt with God standing behind us. The Yes from God is enough. The Devil doesn't care when you sit at home and watch football on a Sunday, but you better believe he is crafty and deceptively moving to doubt you when you put one foot in front of the other to have an impact and make a difference. You matter. What you do or don't do matters. Having courage is something I regularly practice in different areas of my life. God has given me a platform on varying degrees over the years and when I go to speak or write, I have these voices that have a field day in my mind trying to thwart what may be helpful for others. I immediately call them out for what they are and quickly remember that God is on the throne and will be with us in battle despite the fear, doubt, and disbelief of who we are created to be.

Recently my husband and I were in a store purchasing a gift for my daughter-in-law for her birthday. I am sure some of you might know this store. Some of you may know this place too well. This particular store gets us and many other people into trouble and we often try and not have our truck with us when we go, if you know what I mean. As we were standing at the checkout line there was a variety of faith-based books. As I was looking at the books, I had this moment of false truth. As I looked at the titles of many of these books, they seemed to be in a similar theme to what I have been writing about thus far. As I stared at the title, my eyes shifted from book to book. An inaudible voice spoke to me, saying that what I have to say has already been said. I questioned what makes my book something others would want to read. Since you are reading this book, I would have to say a resounding thank you for your belief that God can in fact use anyone regardless of what the odds are for effectiveness. Trust God's yes to be the signifying factor of what is most important in His plans for your life. I didn't set out to write it for the massive success of having a lot of people read it. I followed God's lead and that is what mattered. I trust that it will fall on the eyes and ears for those who need it. **Success is not always found in the outcome, it is found in your obedience to His call**.

This Mess has a Message

It is an interesting dichotomy when you go to write words you believe God calls you to write. You truly are at the mercy of the One who made you. With each stroke of the keyboard, it is marginally surreal. I am honored that God has allowed both the mundane AND the supernatural in my life. We cannot however find the supernatural without humility. I am grateful that God gave me the desires and the dreams I have. I am enchanted at the idea that little ole me gets the opportunity to obediently share some excerpts from my life—even the most challenging and difficult ones that have led me to this place. I have a feeling this will continue to unearth emotions in me I never knew existed and will create a space of vulnerability for you to see we are the same yet very unique in our own God-given way.

In the year 1999, my oldest sister became pregnant with her 3rd child in a new marriage. Sadly, for us all, the pregnancy ended abruptly in a miscarriage a few short months later. We grieved deeply. It was an experience that none of us had ever been through. We clung to our faith and trusted God for peace in the loss.

In 2000, I also learned I was pregnant, so Lisa and I were both pregnant together for the first time. It was kind of a big deal in our family for me to be expecting because we had sworn for 6 years that the two boys we had were enough and we never told anyone our plans for a third until we shared the news of our pregnancy. I was so excited to be pregnant at the same time as my sister Lisa, as I had also been pregnant with my other two sisters previously.

On February 14th of 2000, I went in for a routine checkup and learned that I too had miscarried. Now that was gone, along with this precious baby we never imagined we would have a heart for. As I left the doctor's office that day with the announcement of the loss, I had to face my friends and my family. I had to tell them what once was, was now no more. I was so ashamed that my body was no longer carrying this precious life. I had let my husband and kids down. I had let my family down. *Could I ever even get pregnant again? What would people think of me? Was it something I had done?*

As I drove home that day, a song played on the radio. The lyrics were taken from Psalm 23. "Though I walk through the valley of the shadow of death..." *Was this really happening to me?* One of the hardest things I had to go through was repeatedly sharing our loss with others. I could have easily grieved and moved on if no one knew what I was going through, but I had to face my friends and family, and recounting time and again that this pregnancy was no more. My sister, who had been pregnant with me, came over that day and hugged me in a way that no one in my life could hug me. She had recently experienced the same loss. I knew that she KNEW my sadness. It comforted me on a level I never expected.

It's crazy to think that the pain we navigate on this side of eternity can hold so much healing for others. Because of that loss, I too can embrace others having that experience and comfort them in a profound way. While that was a painful time in our lives, God was there and saw us through. I don't know how people can experience the pain and tragedy we are subject to in these bodies *without* the peace and hope that God freely gives us. He is our rock and fortress. He saw us through. We now have an amazing child we would never have had if it weren't for that great loss in our lives. I cling to the hope that one day I will see that baby again and the same peace I have today will wash over me in that heavenly realm. I encourage you to consider and think about what pain you have experienced in your life and how it could be used to help others find hope, healing, and purpose from their tragedy, knowing we can choose to go from pain to purpose.

The Written Word

I have always had awe and reverence for those who write music or books. I have always wondered where they get their inspiration and direction from. We have all had experiences that have left us wounded; where the blood has dried on the wounds. We have a choice to pick ourselves up and say, "God, what do you want me to do with this?" rather than asking "God, why is this happening?" How arrogant is it for us to question the one and only Almighty God, creator of all things, both seen and unseen? Rather, we can choose to allow Him to be glorified in our mess and allow our challenges to be used so that others can come to know Him. So that others can be comforted or encouraged that He is there for us *always*. So much so, that people can know from all walks of life that others have been there before and that we can overcome any obstacle or challenge that comes our way. We make a concerted effort to do all we can to our own ends. We strive for independence and exercise free will, which often leaves us even more bound than we were to begin with. Instead what if we obediently shared the hidden treasures of challenge, and the secret gifts of hardship in the unfolding of this beautiful script we call this side of eternity?

Words of Mass Destruction

Words either connect or correct. Just because we feel compelled sometimes to say something, doesn't mean it should be said. I have heard people say, "I feel better now that it's off my chest." What words may free *us*, might burden, hurt, and enslave another captive? God came to set us free. He didn't say "go and be free." He sent his Son to die in our place and that demonstrative act of love is what set us free. Words are free and they can be used as a weapon of mass benefit or massive destruction. I have shared with you that I have people in my life that have said and shared words with me that have empowered me like lighter fluid to a fire of incredible purpose. Edification with our words can be a firestorm of good or a firestorm of evil.

The tongue is likened to a rudder on a ship and what comes from the mouth is an overflow of the heart. Hurt people, hurt people. God can break the chain of our hurts when we choose to not be in bondage to circumstances or people that hurt us. With our words, we might be able to say something that makes us feel better but, we also have to ask how this will make others feel. That is called being selfless versus selfish. Selfish says how will I feel. Selfless says how will others feel. How we make people feel matters. Showing up for people in some of the most devastating times of their lives is incredible. It's an experience I hope you get to have often. It's a choice you get to make.

We all have the same 24-hours in a day. How we spend our time with others and what we say in those times is incredibly important. There are a lot of insignificant ways we can spend time and I have had my fair share of those as I didn't have a better understanding of my purpose in life. Living a life of significance is critical to finding joy, the joy our lives are intended to embrace. We can see, do, and experience a multitude of fleeting things on this side of eternity. Maya Angelou said, "people will forget what you said, and people will forget what you did. But people will never forget how you made them feel." Our words matter as they equate to how we make people feel. To make ourselves feel better by saying what is on our minds doesn't necessarily equate to something having to be said. When it comes to our nutrition, what we put into our body either helps it heal or it hurts us. The same outcomes can be attached to our words.

If it's not lifting someone else up, we should probably refrain from saying it. Even when we might be "right" in what we are saying, it's better to choose to be in relationship than it is to be right. When we see people as God sees them, we remove our inclination toward criticism. We may be "right" in our evaluation of someone being in error or lacking judgment on their lives, but that doesn't mean it needs to be said. Unless people give us permission to identify areas of their lives that do not align with God's word, it's not our place to say or point it out. It's arrogant for us to assume that other people see things the way we do.

When we choose to see others the way God sees them, we are looking through the lens of grace. I am so grateful for the grace and mercy God extends upon me daily. I choose to have compassion and see others as He sees, whenever I can. Choosing to see others in the same light and mercy as God sees us, releases us from the burden of a critical spirit and the urge to point out other people's shortcomings. We all have them. We all fall short on a daily basis.

When we set out to live a life filled with purpose, we will always encounter people who don't see things the way we do. When people lack confidence in who they are, or what they are created to be and do, they are often the first to be critical of those who are living a life that matters. Living a life that matters can make other people feel insecure, as they haven't yet discovered their true purpose. They may say and do things to thwart your ability to be who God calls you to be. Don't give those people power in your life.

The One who made you knows you the best. When you lay your head on the pillow at night, rest easy, knowing you have performed for an audience of One. When we truly work in service of others, we can rest knowing our work is in line with our purpose. If our motive in serving others is to have others recognize that we are doing good things, we won't be able to find true joy in that service. When I set out to help people in the capacities that I am committed to, I don't need people to thank me or tell me I am doing a good job. I am simply doing what God put in my heart to do. I am not looking to do anything but to please Him and be obedient. Ulterior motives and the expectations of others will only lead to disappointment and a fractured sense of purpose. Yes, your purpose can be known and can be broken. The process of living your purpose can be damaged when we focus on ourselves rather than keeping our aim on our hope to make God famous. We make Him famous by having peace and contentment living the life He intended us to live. That, my friends, is contagious!

I love the idea that when we live out our God-given dreams, we SHOW people that their God-given dreams are possible too! God has uniquely woven parts in your heart that only can be lived by you. When we follow God's calling, we inspire others to do the same. *You* might be the only person in someone's life who will find their purpose and be able to inspire them to live their purpose too. This is critical for you to discover, as other people's blessings are tied to your understanding of this. It's an incredible opportunity to get another layer of peace and satisfaction of living the life God intended for you to live versus a life the world says you should live. We can be easily distracted by the behavior and action in the world and its standards in comparison to what capacity is ordained by God.

Woe is me. Please know that I share these hopefully thought-provoking ideas from a place of humility. I am grateful for where I have been, even in the tough times. I am grateful for who I am and where I am going. I am the "in the trench with you" kind of girl. No matter where you are, guy or girl, or where you have been or what you have been through, we all put our pants on one leg at a time. I value you and I don't even know you. Can you imagine how much more God values you when He created you with purpose, for purpose, and on purpose? We are all unique. God doesn't have the same plans for each of us. God knows that my life partner is very different than I am but that together we are better, and we complement one another with our differences.

Remember that you are your own private label, an original, just as I am. What I have shared with you is simply to provoke thought and possibly implement in some aspects of your life that are more profound, and ultimately, what you were created for. Remember that I am writing out of obedience. Your motive to act on what God has created you to do and be are equally valuable, though it may look very different than what He has assigned to me.

You will find much hope and peace when you seek Him for what your purpose looks like for you on a daily basis. Some days are completely ordinary; others extraordinary. During some "ordinary" days, I reach people in ways I never even knew were possible and the only explanation is God. You can, too. It's never too late to fight for who you are and what it is that God can do in and through you as a vessel. Please take some time and prayerfully consider more of what God planted in your heart; perhaps something you would have never considered to be fruitful can be so. Ask Him what your life of significance looks like. My discoveries have all been works of progress and decisions to propel myself forward, even in my failures.

Confession is good for the soul. If there were a time or two in my life I wish I could go back and erase words or actions, I would choose not to. My failures shape me. I have had words with people that I am remiss were said. But because the outcome was grave, I learned in a profound way to never let those kinds of words be released in that fashion again. There were times when my frustration level in parenting hit the limit and I feared I was desperately failing. There were also situations where I lacked judgment concerning the ways and timing I had communicated with people in my life that changed the trajectory in ways I never would have anticipated. We never know how the words we might say will be received. Even the best-intentioned words can fall on ears that are operating out of past fears, failures, and rejection. They can be internalized and take you down a path you never saw coming. This is why it's important to really slow down long enough to carefully consider what comes from our lives, in word and deed. The more we are doing and saying things that matter, the less likely we are to mess it up.

Most of the instances I regret were times where I was operating with of a high level of fear. Where there is fear, there is absence of love. A good question to ask yourself in such times is, *Are these words or actions rooted in fear or are they rooted in love? Are they selfish or selfless?* The more we prayerfully consider the life God has in store for us, the more He is likely to show us with complete clarity what we should say and do. Our ability to be agents of change is one thousand percent fueled and executed by our Almighty Creator. We are the vessel and He is to direct our course. When we veer off course, it's because we've let fear sneak in. He can help us course-correct and return to our path.

Chapter 3: The Pain has a Purpose

As I began this book, I was just a few short weeks of turning the ripe young age of forty-six. I have been married to my best friend for twenty-five years. Do the math here with the kids' ages, and you'll see we were doing things our way, with our timing rather than God's best for our lives. Our three boys are twenty-six, twenty-four, and eighteen. I don't look back on any experience with regret. I simply look to learn and grow. It truly doesn't make sense to look back when that is not the direction we are heading. I don't know about you, but since I am not perfect, I certainly can't identify with people who have the appearance of perfection. When we see things as perfection, it's just simply an illusion and not a reality. I am one to promote progress over perfection. I like celebrating victories as we grow and learn from the lessons we didn't have epic levels of success with. Generally, my best choices lined up with what God's best was for my life and the ones that weren't so epic were the ones where I operated out of fear and disobedience.

My foundation is strong. My parents raised us with biblical truths, foundation, and clarity for what we could align our lives with—God's best. Which brings me to a great lesson for those of you raising families and who live and worry about doing a good enough job. What matters is that we can lay our head on the pillow at night knowing we taught our kids right from wrong by biblical standards. From their early years we took them to places and gave them experiences where they could find a foundation that mattered.

A dear friend, who also happens to be our Pastor, has spoken some of the most impactful words of truth and teaching into my life over the years. He came into my life at a time when I was hungry and ready. *The student was ready, and the teacher appeared.* I admire Pastor Dan so much. He has lived a life that has not been easy. Being called into ministry is not an easy calling. In fact, some of the most profoundly gut-wrenching times of his life have generated a tremendous amount of fruit in mine. *I would like to think that I would be honored and grateful to have a life that was lived out in a way that was hard for me but that produced tremendous fruit and growth for others.* I believe God allows the pain we go through for purpose. Clearly, he has been through a lot so that others could be taught in a way that exudes passion for the cause. We have choices in life. We can become a victim, or we can become a victor. It's impossible for victims to have success.

I don't know about you, but I want to consider my life a life well-lived, a life lived in a manner worthy of my faith, and a life in which my pain was for the benefit of others. Who you surround yourself with matters. Choose wisely.

Something that I have valued over time as I lead a life of faith is to have the people in my circle that are life-breathing, God-fearing, Bible-teaching Christians. One of my favorite ways to get through a day is to have positive Christian music playing in our home or in the car. There are so many life stories, lessons, and recounts of biblical proportions that have inspired others to put pen to paper with notes and lyrics that we can find solace in. I am in awe of the level of talent people are afforded when they too follow the desires God puts in their hearts to sing and to write music. I find it to be daily counsel of wise words with melody that plays throughout my day. It's hard to be unhappy or ungrateful when you are listening to such encouraging lyrics that generate such hope. I have found that no matter what is happening in my day, that music is still ministering to me even if it's on a subconscious level. I do recommend feeding your soul throughout the day; just as you nourish your body with food, to nourish your soul with uplifting music and scripture. It's amazing the difference in our perspective as we navigate a rather challenging landscape of brokenness, if our hearts and minds are focused on what is good, what matters and God.

God's Life Plan

We made our best effort at those times to show our children the way they should go. They know the direction they need to go to receive more of God's blessing in their lives. We have done our part. We didn't always offer the best examples, but we definitely showed them where they could go and learn God's plan for how to live it. They could see God's mercy and forgiveness demonstrated as we made our mistakes, and how God still cared for us—despite our shortcomings. Ultimately our kids will make the choices they make based on what they know to be their faith and we will be okay with that. It doesn't mean we did a bad job if they make less than desirable choices.

One of the most powerful recommendations I can give you is to pray for your children. Be specific with the prayers. Never stop praying. God hears you and He is faithful to give us what we need, knowing they are His children. I truly believe this had impact to our oldest son marrying his wife. I prayed for her long before she was ever considered. Her relationship with him and our family and her family were covered in years of petitioning God that the perfect mate for him would come into his life. This is probably one of the more significant prayers that God has already answered for me. Oh, how important and powerful our conversations with God are!

Motherhood and marriage have always been two of my greatest joys in life. Some of my deepest, darkest, and most challenging times of my life were from the years 2003 to 2013. As you know, having good health matters. I had a ten-year battle with an illness that falls into the category of autoimmunity. If you are not familiar with autoimmunity, some of the more common diagnoses are Multiple Sclerosis, Fibromyalgia, Lupus, Graves', Crohn's, and Celiac. Mine was called Hashimoto's. It's an autoimmune illness that attacks the thyroid gland in a way that makes it less to non-functional, inciting the need for hormone therapy for what the body isn't producing. When your body is attacking itself, there are a lot of inflammatory processes associated with it. Inflammation equates to fatigue, pain, and overall very little desire to do much of anything, including smile. This illness took away my ability to be the best wife and mother I could be. I fought hard for ten years and God afforded me healing with nutrition and spiritual practices. I needed some really good supplementation to help repair the imbalance our North American Western diet had undone.

Over the past six years I navigated on a new journey that had me pondering *what now*? I knew that God allowed the sting of my illness to be present and real for the time He allowed for a purpose. My pain = His purpose. I also realized that I was to have a platform to help others overcome similar health issues. I had done it in a way that was truly by trial and error. While a lot of what we tried on the Eastern side of medicine, with a more holistic approach, failed to generate the healing I had desired and fought for, it was a daunting pursuit for ten years. I had just enough hope in this process and knew I was fighting on purpose for a purpose.

A Blessed Perspective

As time progressed, I came to a place where I began to have more wins than losses. There is a lot to be said about the value of operating out of hope to keep up the good fight. I had been born an introvert by nature. I believe this can be a crutch for some. As a child of God, it was limiting for me to claim to be a self-professed non-engaging person. While I know personality types are general inclinations, I believe that we can choose ways to make that inclination more or less impactful, while maintaining a significant amount of purpose. I can see some advantages to being on the quieter side, as it allows for others to talk more than you and when we listen long enough, we find a place of learning who others are, and makes our ability to connect with others all the more powerful.

I also knew that if God was giving me a platform to help others, I was going to have to do some growing too. This helped me see more clearly who God truly designed me to be rather than claim a propensity to a behavior that could limit who I was created to be. I have read many books over the years. Some of them have been life altering for my ability to see who I am, and I believe that if God gave me a platform, He would and could use me the most if I were to become more like Him.

Recently I read a book, and after reading the first few chapters, I immediately connected with the message. Mostly because it was real, authentic, and darn right vulnerable. I mean, seriously in my wildest dreams, I would never EVEN consider or think about the level of vulnerability that this author had. In fact, since starting my own book, the thought has crossed my mind that I may be led to share in a similar way in order to connect with others and that frightens me to the core. Lord help me, as being vulnerable means being exposed. What was interesting for me to experience is that she shared on a very vulnerable level and no one died as a result of her vulnerability. In fact, she is the most sought out speaker currently on the self-help/faith-based circuit and has been able to connect and have impact on so many lives due to that level of vulnerability she speaks to.

One of my biggest fears in life is the fear of being misunderstood. Being authentic and vulnerable in life is a place for real connection.

I do truly desire authentic connection and hope and pray that I can be taken to that place regularly. As hard as it is, vulnerability is really where hearts collide for connection. God uses those fresh exposed wounds as a connecting point to others who need to feel loved and cared for as their wounds also heal. Most people just want to be heard and known. It allows for validation for who we are. We all go through so many profound hardships in life that it is a powerful place to be able to connect and heal with others as they have been in the same place.

A few years ago, my husband and I did a study by a well-known Christian author and pastor, Frances Chan. The premise of the book is written to bring light to what God intended with marriage. We knew God was working in our lives in profound ways and it was He who brought us together. Clearly, we needed all the good counsel we could get to know His plan for our relationship. We set out for the idea of self-help to learn more of what we could do to make our marriage better.

There are so many unrealistic expectations for the institution of marriage that many people miss experiencing the true meaning of what God intended. We often look to our mate for a certain level of happiness, but ultimately our institution by design is for holiness. This idea that two are better than one is for the purpose of furthering the kingdom of God. It was in that study that I began to realize my happiness in my marriage would be found in becoming holy and leading other people into a relationship with Jesus. What did this look like for Eric and I as a couple? I don't consider myself to be evangelical so how was that going to play out? What kinds of behaviors and activities could be done together as one that were both glorifying to God and had impact on others? This whole concept was edgy and, honestly, very freeing at the same time. It took a lot of pressure off things we had been trying to do to make our relationship better. The answer all along was to follow His ways and tell people about Jesus.

We began praying and seeking more of what these callings would look like. In the study it talked about how the two could be better than one to help care for orphans and widows. Being that we still had a family we were raising and logistically we had space for either, we began seeking the possibility of foster care in our local community. We filled out the beginnings of paperwork and then we had a major move come to play that forced some immediate attention in a different direction. Once we settled our move, we were still feeling called to pursue this avenue. We went to the local foster care system for our county and obtained the mounds of paperwork required for the process. During this time, we were praying, and seeking, and wondering what this would look like for us.

As we dug through the paperwork, we learned that we couldn't have water features on the property unless they were gated. Our new home had a large pond with fish as well as an in-the-ground hot tub. Logistically it would be just short of impossible to gate and fence both water features and were now tasked with a closed door on this possibility. While I still believe there may be the likelihood in our future if we ever moved, we have tabled the idea for now. I say this to point out that as we seek God and grow in marriage, we should always prayerfully consider what it is that God has for marriage for us as we seek the reason the two became one for His plan.

No Barriers to God's Plan

My ten-year battle with Hashimoto's disease robbed me of many of the good moments of my marriage and motherhood. I don't believe I was a terrible friend or negligent to any other outside relationships, but there was something deep inside of me that KNEW God had a big plan for me. I had a hard time wrestling with this knowledge, as I felt physically awful on a regular basis. I had high levels of inflammation as part of the illness and significant fatigue. When I received my diagnosis, my boys were ten, eight and two. I had symptoms for some time before that, but it was a defining day when I finally was diagnosed.

It was with that new knowledge I began a fight. I was not interested in a pharmaceutical solution or a temporary Band-Aid. I was not good with "there is no cure" and "here is the medication you will need to take for the rest of your life." I knew God had the ability to use as a tool to help others, me despite my illness. I continued to do all the things I needed to do in daily life, with a manufactured smile, and the hope for a resolution to my illness. I selfishly prayed for relief from my illness, and felt almost all hope for my recovery was lost.

I had tried so many avenues to heal, including a very strict diet to no avail. Most people would have never known the battle I was facing on a daily basis. I am not one to complain so I just dealt with it silently for the better part of ten years. Even the people closest to me didn't truly know the magnitude of my struggle, including my husband and kids. It would come up on occasion with friends, as there were certain foods I was refrained from eating. This raised questions when people would have us over for dinner, or when we would go to a restaurant with friends and I would ask how certain food was prepared and what the ingredients were. And while it was challenging, it still seemed selfish to talk about as I knew there were plenty of people in life navigating much more difficult health situations than I was.

I am incredibly grateful for the capacity to hope. Hope is an enigma: it is faith in the unseen and unknown for improvement in whatever area of life is suffering. When all hope is lost, the ideas of purpose and meaning in everything quickly escape us. Hope is something we champion inside ourselves. *We choose for hope to always be present.* We choose how we see our situations. We become more powerful in purpose when we choose hope in anticipation of God's greater purpose for our lives.

Generally speaking, people who read a lot are quite intelligent and wise, as wisdom often follows knowledge. Applying this wisdom takes what we learn that creates impact and generates a powerful ripple effect. I have read a lot of books over the better part of the last twenty years. Unfortunately, I don't have the best recall or commitment to memory that I wish I had. I remember a lot of things in generalities. I am not a super detail-oriented person as some are in the area of specific recall. I skim and evaluate concepts and ideas based on what is most important. There are many books I pick up and cannot finish, and some I pick up and can't put down. They either capture me right away or they quickly lose me. I either immediately connect or I don't.

I am an encourager of others. It saddens me to look into people's eyes and see despair. I see people in a way that they don't see themselves and I value pouring into them, the words of life about who God created them to be. When prompted to speak hope into people, these great words of God-given wisdom flow from my lips, followed by a moment of self-reflection on God's amazing grace. It is an incredible feeling to be a vessel of words for others, just like my grandfather revealed to me that day twenty years ago.

I also have what I would consider to be a spiritual gift: the gift of intuition. I study people's mannerisms and words and get a "gut feeling" when something good or bad is happening in their lives. It is a great gift to have as a mother, but not so great for teenage boys when your mom has this super ninja power, we also refer to as the

Holy Spirit. I can distinctly recall times I learned things about my boys, and when confronted, they would look at me in amazement and wonder how on the earth I found out about it. Eric would bring clarity for them and say, "You know your mom is in tight with the Holy Spirit, right?"

I didn't learn everything my boys did that wasn't in line with God's plan for their lives and I am okay with that. I believe God exposes sin that needs to be exposed. I am also grateful that there are things about me that my parents never learned of either. We will mutually take those to the grave. Sometimes my boys, who are now in their 20's, will start to tell me things that I didn't know and I will kindly plug my ears, close my eyes, start humming a tune, and tell them that I don't want to see them any differently for decisions they made when their brains weren't fully formed. I like to think that God has an unsuspecting skewed view of us as well, but in a way that is to our advantage. *He forgives and forgets and sees who we are becoming rather than the choices we have made in the past that weren't always honorable to Him.* His grace washes freely over all of us and he operates with us in a way that we can learn from others.

Our bodies are amazing vessels. It is incredible to see and feel a transformation like I have over the last five years and the different point of view I operate under on a daily basis, as I become more and more whole. I knew my vessel was broken when I got my diagnosis in 2003. It's still broken and will be until I am with Jesus one day. But for now, there are a lot less cracks.

Healing, from the Inside Out

In 2013, my body began to heal in profound ways. I was trying new ways to heal from the inside out. It was like a treasure chest was being opened. I began to see this incredible platform to help others heal. This healing gave me fresh eyes to see more of what God could do in and through me. I was grateful for what was unfolding. I didn't want to be selfish and not help others heal, when I clearly had found a progression of steps to heal that was working for me. I had a profound sense that what I was doing could also help others. Of course people would want to hear what I have to say that could help them feel better! *Helping people heal and to see who God created them to be through that healing is an experience I am so grateful to have.* We need more of that happening in all of us. **I need you to understand that no matter where you are, or what you have been through, it is for a purpose**. There are people who need to be held by you. There are people who need to know that God is in control and that any circumstance, any tragedy, or disaster is something that can be used to help. Be there for people. What you are going through, have gone through, and will go through matters.

I have a friend who used to live close to our church. Before she moved, I invited her several times to come to church and she agreed multiple times. In my past invites she would respond with her fear that the church would burn down if she came. I don't think her thoughts are unique. I believe a lot of people think or feel that they aren't good enough to come to church. Church is a place where we go to learn how to be more Christ-like. It's an intentional place where we gather as a community to fellowship with people who are all on the same page, desiring a connection and relationship with God and with others. Church is a place where you can come and go, and you are welcomed and loved.

A few years ago, we had a message series at church that was titled "Matters." The series message was on the church billboard for weeks. My church burning-down-fearing friend sent me a picture of her new license plate with the word MATTERS as her personalized plate. God weaves people into our lives on purpose. I hope and pray that we are living a life that is passionate about what matters. She matters. We all matter.

When I was in the throes of my illness, I muddled through and got by. I did the best I could within the confines of illness and self-proclaimed introversion. In fact, many people never even knew I was sick. I didn't talk about it much. I am not a complainer by nature. I am also not a victim. I was obedient and answered the call to do a lot of things that normally would have been outside the scope of what health issues were holding me back, but God held me. I KNEW I was being held and I allowed Him to hold me. I allowed Him to use me in that state.

It wasn't at my best, but He was sufficient for me in that season of life. One area of ministry that I felt called to at the time was the Children's Ministry. I was raising kids and it was helpful to learn stories from the Bible that I could relate to my own kids as well. How hard could it be, right? I mean, they were five and I was thirty-ish. Clearly, I could faith it until I made it. They say if you want to learn something, to teach it. Teaching those kids taught me a lot. It taught me how simple God's love is and how easily it can be communicated. The answer is Jesus, so not a whole lot of multiple choice or essay questions to create confusion.

What is interesting to look back on now is how clearly I remember how I felt physically and how God still used me. What was important was that I answered the call and He equipped me to go. I didn't need to be whole or perfect; I needed to be willing even though, by my standards, I didn't feel whole enough to be helpful. I can now see the value in the capacity God used me and the impact I have as He continues to call and equip me at higher levels of influence.

We all grow in our capacity to live a life of significance—by choice. Once we see who we are, we can walk with a tremendous amount of purpose. Typically, God doesn't take us from infant to adult. We have the wonder years, where we learn and grow and mature into obedient children who have nothing but gratitude for the precious gift of life and eternity beyond. The only explanation for how I made it through that time in my life was by moving from miracle to miracle and His amazing grace, how sweet is that sound.

I was taught by a wise man at a conference that we often focus on goals in life, yet these goals can restrict our capacity for higher levels of success. It's in our nature to hit a goal, then withdraw. We become complacent, unwilling to raise the bar, and go for the next goal because the last one was hard. We become discouraged that the next one will be even more difficult, maybe unattainable.

Goals often hinder us, as we will limit certain things that are helpful to reach those goals. For example, if you have your own business and you want to ramp up sales, you might put on a big sale, which requires more resources like time, money for advertising, energy, and effort, rather than devote your time to mindless activities like watching television. Even weight loss goals can be counterproductive as we typically deprive ourselves of a variety of foods to achieve our weight loss goals. Yet, all we do is simply go back at the end of the goal and make up for the lost time for what we sacrificed by shrinking back and becoming complacent.

My mantra in life is *progress over perfection*. I believe we are most productive when we have a plan for growth, rather than a goal. Growth plans are progressive and not limiting. We are always making small changes, small baby steps in a progressive manner that isn't limiting but gives us the ability to never arrive. We never arrive in our humanity. But we can always make small changes over time that are simple, effective, and long lasting for the growth of it all.

One part of my practice as a holistic health coach that gives me tremendous joy and peace is to help people heal from the inside out, helping them see their lives with clarity and conviction, and to experience life on God-sized playing field. The impact we can have when our vessel has fewer cracks is limitless. There are things that can seep out of those cracks when we are not the best version of ourselves, that can take away from our ability to do the most with the time we have been given. I feel so honored and grateful to share and write no matter where this goes or whose eyes they fall upon. To have what I have and even think about saying what God has done in and through me over the years with the gift of healing I have been given. A person who has their health has a thousand dreams. A person who does not, has just one—that is to feel better. Most people have no idea how good they are designed to feel, and most people don't even know what they are capable of doing until their vessel is whole.

Gratitude is a practice of receiving a gift that keeps on giving. When we stop and consider what we each have that we can be grateful for, it's an incredible change of perspective. It is life altering. Our minds tend to wander and think about what we don't have, as we constantly strive to fill our lives with things that don't matter. I have never been one to think about this topic on grandiose levels until the last five years. Those who are ungrateful fail to see what is ideal. They see what they don't have and that is their focus. It's hard for me to be ungrateful when I have two hands to write, two eyes to see, two ears to hear, and a healthy heart that beats with passion for life eternal and for the process of having purpose. I knew that if I could operate out of as much gratitude for my salvation, that I could move mountains, to tell others about the hope I have for just about anything. I also knew that if I could be grateful for the health restoration I had been given, I had to ante-up. I value helping people heal so they can see more of what it is that God puts in their hearts in service to Him. I don't believe we are given such amazing gifts for our mouths to be closed or for our bodies to not be used for the glorification of God.

When Eric and Caleb read the book *The Dream Giver* with me a few years back, one of the things I shared with them was this God-sized dream that I felt I had in my heart to be present with people during a disaster. Disaster seemed to happen to so many people and put them in a place of helplessness. I know God created me to help. As I watched tragedies unfold on the news, I was compelled to be a part of a relief effort. Salvation Army, Red Cross, you name it, I could see myself being a part of it. But it seemed inconceivable when you have a family counting on you to take care of them.

Would I pick up and just go help someone else when I had responsibilities to care for my immediate family? It was a chasm I couldn't bridge. Why would I have this desire if I didn't actually have the ability to do it?

Chapter 4: Washoe Drive Fire

In January of 2012, I got a call one morning from my son Caleb, who was eleven at the time. He was calling from school, saying that there was a fire in the area, and that they were evacuating all the children to another school nearby. This was also very close to our home.

I was not at home when he called. I was at a store seven miles away getting paint for our dining room. I quickly dropped everything and drove home to retrieve our dogs and evacuate. I got a call from my husband, a police officer, who had been on a treadmill doing his annual stress test. He said he had received word of the fire in our neighborhood right before he arrived at the doctor's office. The technician conducting his stress test said, "You are free to go, because your heart rate is already off the charts." He told me he was headed home in his police car. It had already taken me forty-five minutes to travel what normally would have taken me three minutes. We were terrified our dogs wouldn't make it out in time. We both raced home as quickly as we could.

Debbie is a longtime family friend. We met many years before the fire, when we worked as adult leaders of our church youth group. Debbie has known Caleb from a young age and holds great affection for him. Anyone who meets Caleb knows he is not like most kids. He is a quiet, gentle spirit and has always had this amazing connection with our Creator.

The morning of the fire, as he was getting ready for school, he was singing *Amazing Grace* out loud as he walked around the house. This was the first time he had done something like this, so I found it odd, but endearing. I texted Debbie that morning, and told her what he was singing and how sweet it was.

It was just a few short hours later that I received the call from Caleb, that fire was quickly spreading through our neighborhood. *Our neighborhood? Seriously, was this happening in our neighborhood? Fires just don't happen in our area!*

As I raced home from the store that day, the traffic at the junction just three miles from our house was blocked off, as a presidential candidate had been in town campaigning that day. The roads were also blocked in other directions due to the evacuations. I remember thinking to myself how frustrating it was that this candidate's presence was impeding my ability to get to our dogs and save them from the fire.

It Was a Prayer of Protection

When I finally reached the intersection, I was able to show identification of my address and they allowed me in my neighborhood. What an incredibly creepy 3-mile drive that was, through the smoke, not knowing if our home was still standing or if our beloved dogs were still alive. I was comforted to know that our boys were safely at school and no one was home, but I desperately needed those dogs to be alive. I don't know about you, but our dogs are like our children.

As I drove down our street, I could see flames on both sides of the road through the thick smoke. I pulled the car in the driveway and ran inside to find our precious dogs resting peacefully, without a care in the world! I was able to grab them and quickly left our home, not knowing whether it would be standing the next time I returned.

Thankfully, we were spared the travesty many other families faced on their return. Thirty houses were burned in our neighborhood that day and sadly, one life was lost. We had about $60,000 worth of smoke damage and my son's '67 mustang burned in our driveway. After the smoke cleared, Debbie sent me a message, asking, "Do you realize that Caleb prayed a hedge of protection around your home that day, by singing Amazing Grace?"

The day after we were evacuated to a hotel, we returned to our home. They technically weren't allowing anyone back in the neighborhood but with Eric's connections, we got in. It was January and there was a storm coming through. They predicted there would be flooding in our area with the amount of rain being forecast in combination with the now barren landscape in the surrounding hills.

Preparing for the Flood

We had a creek running through the back of our property which had been known to rise to cresting levels, and potentially to flood. We also were "down range" from other properties, and our home had actually flooded a few years before, when the previous owners lived there. After we sandbagged and prepared, all five of us sat huddled by the woodstove in a powerless home waiting for the flood to happen. The potential for rain was obviously welcomed to help put the fire out, but were we really going to experience a fire and a flood in the same twenty-four hours?

It rained and rained that night and the waters rose, but we didn't flood. Knowing our home had previously flooded meant it may happen again one day. There are always events we are subject to in this world, what we think of as inconceivable disasters—and then they happen to us. We are given the ability to process, and move through these events with power and purpose, and knowing that God holds us, no matter what happens. He is our answer of hope to see us through.

One of the lessons I learned in my travels is this idea that when we become subject to something extraordinary, we can be impacted in a way that we become a "victim" to a circumstance. Through most of my early adult years, before I found strength in my faith, I agreed with the doctrine of **lex talionis** —an eye for an eye. It seemed fair to pass on to one what they had dished out to another. It seemed like a great way to stick it to the man and gain satisfaction by seeing a person suffer for what they had made someone else go through. As I have grown in my faith, my thoughts have shifted toward those of grace.

When we had the fire go through our neighborhood, it was started accidentally by an older gentleman putting fireplace ashes into a plastic trash can. He thought they were cold and harmless, but they weren't; days later the trashcan ignited. Our oldest son lost his treasured '67 Mustang. He had just finished rebuilding it but hadn't yet insured it to the level it had been restored to. He wanted to recover his loss by suing the person who started the fire for the damages. While this is a typical response to being hurt, it doesn't mean pursuing this man personally was the most appropriate response in this case.

We all have choices in life. How we navigate through unexpected events is up to each of us. Victims cannot have success. It's important that we seek the path of forgiveness; to see others the way God sees them and to move on in peace. When we harbor anger, bitterness, or resentment, the only prisoner is ourselves. A wise friend once shared with me that we remain stunted at any given stage of growth when we blame someone else for what is wrong in our life.

Chapter 5: Houston

Almost exactly one year ago to the day, at one o'clock in the afternoon on a Sunday, my husband came into my office where I sat tinkering away on my computer. He asked me what was on my calendar for the week. I said I had appointments here and there but nothing too important. I asked him what was up.

"I think we are supposed to go to Houston," he said.

In the summer of 2017, there was a lot of flooding in Texas. It had been happening for a few weeks and it seemed there was no end in sight. The flood waters rose, and the rescues were surreal as we watched from 1,600 miles away. Let me remind you how powerful it is when you speak and bring life to your dreams and you surround yourself with people who are also dream-doers.

Since we became one, we are very connected, often, finishing each other's sentences. The nature of how we connect is interesting, as we are so incredibly different. We do, however, agree on the things that matter most. That's the beauty of celebrating what your mate is not, and knowing that God brings us together to complement one another in our weaknesses and unite us in our strengths. Notice I didn't say that He brought us together as if it's a one-time event. Yes, at one point in time we committed to one another, but it's a constant decision we make to be brought together, as God loves each of us through each other. I love the idea that we don't have to be everything to each other or others around us. But we do come together on what matters most.

Called to Give Back

At the time, we had our then twenty-two-year-old son, Garrett, living with us, who had recently returned home from serving in the military. We sat Garrett and Caleb down and told them we felt called to go help in Houston, and if they could hold down the fort at home. They both quickly agreed. We prayed together and in one hour we were packed and on the road for our sixteen-hundred-mile trek south-east. I quickly realized we would need our friends and family partnering with us in prayer, so we posted our plan on social media. I text a few close family members, including my parents, and let them know where we were headed and why. Within minutes there were hundreds of people cheering us on and confirming our decision and agreeing to pray with us and for us. I had people messaging me with suggestions of places we could go that they knew were in need. When we step out in faith, the floodgates open to help us on our path.

We had met a family on a zip-lining adventure in Cabo San Lucas, Mexico the year before who lived in Texas and had already been evacuated. They made some suggestions and connected us to different organizations that needed help. I had a friend who had a brother living in Houston who was on high ground and they offered us a place to stay. Everything seemed to come together seamlessly as the days unfolded.

What we never anticipated was the fear and doubt that set in as we got further away from home. Were we doing the right thing? Were we really equipped to do a task of this magnitude? Would our family be okay without us?

Overcoming Doubt

We also had concerns about our safety. You name it, floods of negativity, doubt, and concern for making the wrong decision set in with each passing mile. Eric had actually contemplated turning less than an hour after leaving, but because I had shared our story publicly, he felt that there was no turning back. It was frightening and exhilarating at the same time. The farther we got from home, the more committed we became. We were not operating on our strength or ideas, but on God's. The only explanation I can offer for the peace that comes in a decision to step out in faith when you feel called to do the extraordinary is supernatural. When all else doesn't make sense, God is filling in those cracks of doubt and fear, walking with you. He is always there, we simply have to allow Him in to do what He does best, provide for those He calls.

Two days later, as we ascended into Texas from Nevada, I found myself being ministered to in a way that I never imagined. It was humbling to say the least. I was here to minister to those who were hurting and suffering, and here I was, experiencing this indescribable sense of purpose while being ministered to by God himself. We arrived late on a Tuesday and quickly were connected to a local church where we began our service to others. When we set out to help, we didn't know what we could realistically *do* to help. We stopped en route and bought things we thought we might need like, rubber boots and hip-waders. We prayed as we journeyed this unchartered territory, for God to lead us, renewing our confidence that we were doing what we had been called to do.

Samaritan's Purse

Day two found us in Brazos County, southern Texas. We served at a local community center where food, clothing, and household items were being donated and we were sorting through the donations. Service is not always about the bounty we produce when we serve, or the magnitude of what we are able to do. Service is about being available and obedient—and present. While it seemed chaotic, we always felt guided to the next place God wanted us to be.

It was on day three where we partnered with an organization called Samaritan's Purse.

They were organized. They had a method in all the madness, and it worked. We valued their philosophy and we quickly became "day volunteers" with their organization. We were strategically trained and put to work and good use for people who needed most.

I have had some of what I consider to be "powerful experiences" in my life, but they pale in comparison to the experience we are given when we serve others selflessly in their time of need. We are all vulnerable to catastrophes. No one is immune. We must rely on God to show us what good can come from such a tragic situation. Don't get me wrong, we all have choices in how we respond to things that happen, whether within our control or not. We have a choice on how to process accidents, natural disasters, or tragedies of any kind. We can become victims of circumstance or we can choose to be a victor. So much more peace and positive impact comes from being victorious.

By the end of the week we found ourselves logistically being "worked" out of the area close to where we had been staying. Fuel was becoming an issue and housing for us was non-existent due to so many families who had been displaced from their homes. Grocery stores and restaurants were closed. While we were unable to stay as long as we would have liked, we found that the time we did spend there was useful to God in that it ministered to others.

It was inspiring to be with people who had been subject to such loss and have them serving others alongside us. Somehow, tragedy restores my hope in humanity by uniting people for a cause. *If you want to be moved, move mountains with others.*

In all of our disaster relief experiences we got to work with families that were impacted yet were still helping. When a group of 20–30 individuals who show up in their tragic time and say they want to help, a heavy load is quickly lifted by the power in numbers.

If you have moved house in your life, you've had a glimpse of what it feels like to have people show up in what seems to be an overwhelming time. It can quickly be mitigated by more hands on deck; not just the physical aspects, but the psychological ones as well, when we feel like we are alone in our toil. We have the means to lighten other people's loads simply by showing up in their lives and saying, "I am here for you."

One of the neat experiences disaster survivors also get to have is when we all stand in a circle and pray for them. Whether people are faith-based or not, who wouldn't want to be prayed over? It takes another layer of overwhelm off to know people are petitioning our Creator for peace and help for them in this difficult time. They also get to hear where the volunteers are from. Some are neighbors and then others, like us, drive for days to them in their time of need.

Speak Your Dreams

A worthy phrase that you may hear me say over and over in this book is that it's powerful to speak your dreams. It's also powerful to speak them as they are unfolding and to be surrounded by people who believe in you; by those who are your biggest fans when you step out in faith. *Encouraging words are powerful.*

As I drove to meet a friend today, I pondered the idea of what my hope would be for this book. *What is my message? What do I want people to know?* I have found in our travels, and as we step out in faith, that people love to be *inspired.* I know there are a lot of motivational people and circumstances that have played key roles in becoming who I am today. So many of us get caught up in the mundane that we fail to see the bigger picture of why we are here, why we go through the challenges we do, and why all of that matters most on this side of eternity.

A friend of mine passed away a few years back. She was young by most standards. She was one of the first people I knew personally who was diagnosed with terminal illness and quickly passed on to be with Jesus. To watch her navigate her last days and how she chose to spend them spoke to me. Life is precious and short. We are not promised tomorrow. We often miss-use our time, we fail to see the gravity of how quickly it disappears. I have sometimes pictured what my funeral would look like. *Would people say I lived well? Would they say I loved well? Would they say they knew what my faith-life was? Would they think of me as having lived a life that mattered?*

This past summer, three books collided into my daily quiet/ personal growth/prayer time. One of them was a Bible study on the book of Philippians, with the title *What Matters Most*. Another was a book that a friend had recommended to me, and the minute she sent me the picture of the book cover, I immediately purchased it on Amazon, called, *Come Matter Here*. The third book, *Girl Wash Your Face,* was the first book I started to read and had a hard time setting down. Reading it actually compromised personal hygiene some days. This girl was SPEAKING to ME! I have read a lot of books over the years. I knew that if God was giving me this God-sized platform, I was going to have to grow in BIG ways! *Girl Wash Your Face* inspired me to do EVEN bigger things that I had ever imagined.

I don't believe in chance and I don't believe in coincidence. I believe that our lives are supposed to be **with purpose, for purpose, and on purpose**. The sooner we figure out what those things are, the sooner we discover the point to it all. What I want you to know is that God can use *everyone*, regardless of past, present, or future. He always has and always will. *Ask Him what He wants you to do with your life and watch as He provides you the opportunities that line up with His desires. God doesn't give us dreams that match our budgets. He isn't checking our bank account. He is checking our faith.*

Chapter 6: The Saddest Place on Earth

Have you ever heard that saying, *go with your gut feeling?* Upwards of 70% of our immune system stems from our gut. They call the human gut our "second brain." It's a powerhouse for the human body. I lived with a compromised immune system for ten years. I was often sick and had a lot of food sensitivities or intolerances. At one point I was completely gluten, corn, pork, and dairy free, with minimal sugar consumption. The gluten felt like razor blades going through my system. With the others I simply felt ill when I ate them, so I kept them to an absolute minimum. I could only eat eggs if they were without hormones or antibiotics; otherwise, unspeakable things unfolded.

Since my food list was limiting, I often ended up cooking one meal for me, and a different meal for the rest of my family. Back then we didn't have the healthy food variety that we have nowadays.

We have a nerve that runs from our gut to our brain. It transmits signals to the brain, and when the gut is off, oftentimes the imbalance in the brain is indicating we are sad, depressed, or anxious. I was often grieved by the sheer volume of what I couldn't eat, that it was overwhelming and all consuming. I was anxious and constantly navigating emotions that would appear to be handled through the faith and hope I have, but when you have a physiological imbalance, the magnitude is much larger than most would imagine. It would seem that your life circumstances would indicate green lights when on the inside you were very much sitting at a red light. There is even shame for people who have faith when battling anxiety, sadness, or depression.

What many fail to know is that the imbalance in many instances is a physiological imbalance and often a direct result of the food we eat that creates an imbalance in the gut, sending a signal to the brain saying we are "off." Since 70% of the immune system is rooted in the gut, and my immune system was compromised, I often struggled with anxiety and sadness. This kind of imbalance happens on the inside and needs to be fixed at the root level or it progressively will get worse. Pharmacology doesn't address the root cause. There is a time and place for pharmacy, but it simply provides a way for our symptoms to be less obvious.

Depression and Anxiety

Depression and anxiety are very real. They are gripping our society. As a society, we have lost hope on so many levels: physically, spiritually, and emotionally. The level of despair seems and feels unrecoverable. There is no shame in it. The only shame is that we don't address it on the variety of levels it can, and should, be addressed. Happiness is an inside job. Logistically, it's a body out of balance with what the gut is transmitting to the broken brain. It's a level of despair that the enemy has a hold on us that seems unshakable.

I am here to tell you as someone who has come from this place, that there is hope from the depths of despair. Not only do we lose lives daily to the despair depression causes, we lose people while they are in this place when we can help release them sooner and get them onto the path of doing more of what matters. An author of a book I recently read dealt with this on a very real level. One good thing turns into another. She chose to focus her time on what matters, which was helping others even in the depths of her own despair. She did small mundane tasks that were mindless to her, but helpful to others. The more she focused on others, the less she had time to focus on herself and with a lot of prayer, healthier nutrition, and right actions, she too, recovered.

A Holistic Approach

As a holistic approach, I value taking a step back and evaluating the whole picture of what we are struggling with, from the inside out. I often try to relate this idea of "holistic" as it means to look at the whole picture. There is often more than meets the eye. Many times, when we make poor food choices, it is because we are working a job we don't love, and probably not making money to cover what we need. This leads to struggling relationships and then we eat poorly when we think about those imbalances in our life. It becomes a series of unfortunate events that spool into behavior that is undesired and a lifestyle that is misaligned with who we are designed to be. Another great example of how I see things is if I have an unfortunate encounter with another person, I will assume that something has happened in their day or even in their life that has put them in this negative frame of mind. There is always more to a story.

This gives me the ability to have a LOT more grace and mercy for other people. I have had my fair share of inappropriate communications with people who have said and done hurtful things to me. People who "love" you shouldn't be treating you this way. I tend to offer a lot more grace to those who love me because I know there is hurt somewhere in their life, not directly related to me. It's more about what is happening to them. People will love you, or hate you, and it has nothing to do with you. Look at the "whole picture." You can say, "I am sorry that you are hurting, and I love you. Is there anything I can pray about specifically for you?"

I Feel your Pain

By nature, I am what is commonly referred to as an empath. If you are not familiar with the curse/blessing of empathy for others, as empaths, we take on the emotions of others, as well the emotions we carry in our own souls. For example, if I am at a funeral for someone I am not close to, my emotions are moved to feel what they are feeling. I will take on the emotion of their grief.

When I was growing up, in middle school I was so worried about fitting in. Having the right clothes, the right friends, the right experience, as we were advancing through the wonder years while closely mimicking alien life. Middle school is a time in my life I WISH to I could erase. I absolutely hated it.

When I was in elementary school, I had a fairly good grasp on who I was but that quickly changed in middle school. I can picture the day I went to the school nurse and she gave me antacid so my stomach wouldn't be doing so many flip-flops from my nerves. I didn't give it a lot of thought at the time, but when I look back, I can see how it was the beginning something starting to surface in my life. One of my biggest fears is my fear of being misunderstood. I have what I would consider to be a great heart. I love God. I love others. I value living my life in a way that matters. But people who lack clarity and confidence in who they are, can be downright awful. How we are perceived by others matters, it is either validating or crippling.

I was at a conference once and in the restroom during break, another woman complimented me on my shirt. It had the word "Slim" written in little tiny jewels. As I was washing my hands and looking into the mirror at her as she was exiting the restroom, she said that she liked my shirt and I thanked her for her kind words. She proceeded to tell me as she walked out the door that her dad used to call her *Fatty Patty* when she was growing up. And then, I thought about what my dad used to call me in my adult years. He called me *Slim* or *Slim Jim*.

I wasn't chubby when I was growing up, but I was a little larger than a lot of my peers. After having three kids and having the autoimmune illness that compromised my ability to have a healthy weight despite diet and exercise, he still affectionately referred to me as *Slim*. Words matter. Be careful how you speak to and about yourself. Be careful what you speak about others to them. Remember that it takes ten positives to counteract one negative.

Worry Gets You Nowhere

Worry is like a rocking chair: it keeps moving but doesn't get you anywhere. Corrie ten Boom had such wise words for us. There are so many things in life that can take us out of comfort zones, things that God wants to show up for us and be what we need to be to accomplish His plans for good. When I was growing up I used to be a serious nail biter. I had a lot of shame associated with it. It wasn't a pretty site and I was embarrassed by it. But I did worry. I worried mostly about how I was being perceived. *Was I a good student? Was I going to graduate high school? Was I "Christian enough?" Was I pretty enough? Was I someone others wanted to be around?* A place I could go to think about all of these things, was biting and biting. Thinking and biting got me nowhere. Worry doesn't change a thing.

This morning I was reading in Philippians 4:6-7 and the question was asked in my study book: *What word in this passage stood out the most?* The word *anything* was resonating. Do not be afraid about ANYTHING, but in every situation by prayer and petition, present your requests to God. The peace of God surpasses all understanding, and will guard your hearts and your minds. Sounds pretty all encompassing, doesn't it? What exactly does anything entail? Oh, you mean what others think about you? Yes. Oh, you mean will others misunderstand me? Anything and Everything IS all encompassing. So why then do we still do it? Control? Fear? Or dare I say….*pride?* We have this thing we battle called pride. I have since kicked the habit, for the most part, of biting my nails but I replaced it with another habit that I absolutely despise that I do. I have even contemplated getting hypnotized for it.

Wait, what? *Why have I not turned this over to God? Is it too big? Is it too silly?* It truly is evidence of my worry and fear that I face. I have reduced my habit to picking at the skin around my nails. There, I said it. I feel shame. It's not ideal. Its evidence that I still worry to about what people think of me, what success I am having or not having in life, and whether or not I am doing what truly matters. I pick. I bite. And I don't like it one bit. Sometimes I am just thinking, and I do it. Just with random thoughts I think, and I pick. I feel the skin around my nails for imperfections and if I feel the slightest imperfection where the skin has an unsmooth surface, I am constantly picking at it. My husband often acknowledges it too. He knows I do it. He knows I don't like it. He will often ask me what is on my mind when he sees me picking to help me work through it. I am a pretty good communicator and feel I do a good job at being open with communicating the good, the bad, and the ugly. We still face so many internal battles that are already won. We need to let the King of the world in on every aspect of our lives, so He can show up and do His thing for us. Let Him in whatever it is. I am an overcomer. WE will overcome this.

One of the Best Days of my Life

I advocate for filling in our nutritional gaps with supplements. Our North American Western diet has made us sick. I have found a company with supplements that have helped me heal the root cause issue of my illness. I promote their products in my practice. I have been able to help a lot of people this way. Last year the company asked me to speak on a topic I have done well with. I was honored to speak. I was given some speaking points via teleprompter, but something I felt I had to say which was unscripted and needed to be said first and foremost, is that nothing I accomplish is because of my own skill. I can do what I do *only* because of what God has moved me to do. My ability to be good at it is a God-given talent and a God-given desire to do it to the best of my ability. I also made certain to say that my daily desire is to bring glory to God in whatever I am doing.

That day was one of the best days of my life. It was a platform to share my hope and faith. It was a platform to tell thirteen thousand of my colleagues that we can have so much more impact and effectiveness when God is at the forefront and that He needs to be at the head of all we do. When He is, the rest falls into place. Sharing my faith and what I do in business, has afforded me great success. For someone who values words, my husband shared a public proclamation. He posted about how proud he was of me on his social media feed. I think people who struggle to value who they are, need to hear it from others. It lifts us up. We rise when others recognize who we are. I think deep down we know, but we have to believe it for ourselves. Then we need others to acknowledge us too. It empowers us to move forward even more passionately. We all have good days and bad days. **Be the person who speaks words of life over others**. Words are free. Use them to make a positive difference in the lives of others. They need to hear it from you.

Chapter 7: Change is for the Better

Change is always for the better. It is all how we see it. If you want to see good, you will find the good. If you want to see pain, you will find pain. I love change. Well, let me clarify. I love change that is on my terms. I am the girl who needs a fresh scene, a fresh outlook, a precise change by moving furniture around. It helps me feel like positive is happening in my life. Recently we decided to do an addition on our home. We spent a decent chunk of our hard-earned money to have plans drawn up, and then submitted to the contractor. Our local housing market is booming with a lot of new growth in our area, so the cost of the addition simply was not a good investment. So, instead we decided to work with the space we had. We swapped out our living room and dining room. We have been in our current home for two years. We chose this home because it was only 1/4 of a mile from our oldest son and his wife. Plus, my daughter-in-law's family is right down the street. We are hoping to be grandparents one day and want to be those who are devoted and present as much as we can be. Close proximity sure helps with convenience.

I like convenient. I like simple and effective. However, while the location was ideal, the home did not have the space we were used to. I don't need much space for watching TV and sleeping, but we do like to entertain. We also love to cook, and I feel inspired when I value the space I am in. If I feel I can be creative and cook up something I know people will love, the space I am in matters to me. Our last home had a kitchen remodel and it really inspired our ability to cook better and healthier. We began cooking together and it was a great bonding time. Fellowship and meals with friends and family are memories we create that last a lifetime.

A Soft Place to Fall

Our homes are our soft place to fall. The place we feel valued and the place that matters. Needless to say, it was a lot smaller of a space and we are grateful to work with what we have. Since we have moved things around, when I leave the house and come back, I get great joy thinking about the new space I am coming into and the way it makes me feel. Call me crazy but I love this kind of change. We are also no strangers to the move. In our 25 years together, we have had ten homes. Two were rentals and for shorter periods of time in between home ownership. I hate packing and moving but I do love the change. We have also owned about twice the number of cars as homes we have lived in. I am not a car person per se, but I do value liking what I drive. And I love the fun aspect of owning a new and different car. We are often teased and, dare I say, affectionately shamed by friends about the amount of homes and cars we have owned, but to each his own.

One change I experienced that was outside of my control was when our middle son Garrett went off to the military. Remember that I am an empath? I took it upon myself to take on the emotions of what he would be experiencing in this decision to go and live far away from home and choose a lifestyle that was incredibly risky and often dangerous. His base was on the other coast from us. I remember being incredibly anxious weeks before he left. The day he left I walked into his empty room after he drove away, and I felt like I had been socked in the gut. *Isn't it our job as parents to raise these humans to be independent as they leave to be productive citizens in society? Then why was it so hard for this transition?*

Ain't it Fun...

I remember seeing a post on Facebook about three weeks after he left home, with a video of him post-operative after having his wisdom teeth removed. Whoever drove him home decided to record him and Garrett thought it was equally funny to share this video on Facebook. I remember picking up the phone to text him, "You had surgery and I didn't even KNOW about it? I could have come and stayed with you for the weekend. I could have helped. I could have been there. Why didn't you allow me to be there for you?" And he responded with, "It's not a big deal. I got this."

Then it occurred to me: *Carrie, you raised a human being, he has had a job since he was sixteen-years-old and he is now nineteen. He has driven himself across the country by himself and established a place to live, enrolled in the military, and has now had surgery and has not needed his mom. GOOD JOB! You did it. You raised a productive self-sufficient human being who can be out in society on his own.*

Somehow that realization helped comfort my broken heart and I realized I had done an okay job. This change was good, and it was supposed to happen. He is now back home in Nevada after serving his time and has his own home and has a job! We did okay. This change turned out to be okay.

Our youngest son is in his senior year of high school this year. He has recently been accepted to go to a Christian college in Australia to study pastoral leadership. My initial reaction was, *I could barely do Georgia; how in the world do you think I could handle Australia as the distance between us?* My reaction was to ask if he thought he could actually live that far away from family. His response was, yes, and wouldn't God be His provider for what he needed? Ugh, why do you have to pull the God card on my empath heart? This too will be an okay change.

Don't Lick the Knife

Don't lick the knife. Seems like we are stating the obvious, right? Can I just tell you a few weeks ago in my very kitchen, I licked the BIGGEST, sharpest knife we own after slicing up some avocado? What compels us to do really stupid, obviously bad things? It's in our nature to assume "it" won't happen to us. It happens to others, but it won't happen to us. Fire, hurricane, death, flood, illness, financial setbacks only happens to others. Is that a lie we believe? Is it the enemy setting us up for the opportunity to have the unfortunate unfold in our lives? Bad things happen. Bad things happen to good people. Bad things happen to bad people. We live in a fallen world. We do, however, have free will; the choice we have can have a ripple effect of good or it can have consequence. One good choice turns into another, as does one bad choice.

My travels, Bible studies, and life experiences are filled with people who do things that are ridiculously wrong and make you wonder, why on earth did they do that? The consequences are so obvious. Then there are things that happen as a result of choices others make. Are we to become victim to those choices? Or do we become the subject of those choices? There is a serious fork in the road in these opportunities that we travel that can be used for the good and there is a path we can head down that might not produce the results of having a purpose-filled life. I have always been in awe of people who navigate tragedy with what I would perceive as "well." I remember when I was in my pre-teen years, my uncle Joe went to help a friend roof their house at the base of a mountain. There was a huge mudslide that day, out of nowhere, and it took his life. He had a wife. He had six kids. He was a PASTOR! Why did he need to die?

My aunt was an amazing rock to watch as she navigated this very sad void in her life that was once there, and now gone. She gave God all the credit for her ability to get up each day, even when it was hard. He was there for her. She let Him be there for her. He filled in all the cracks for their family even though the loss was grave, but the empty grave of Jesus told us how this story ends. We will see him again someday, and in the meantime *let our lives reflect the hope we have*. There is a peace God freely gives us that we often refuse to receive. It's always there. He wants to comfort us. He wants to be there for us. **Our lives reflect every choice we make, good, bad, or ugly. We can choose to use these challenges for good or we can choose to become a victim and become ineffective for what God can demonstrate, in and through us, who HE is, in all of it.**

Chapter 8: Stating the Obvious

Last year I was participating in an international non-denominational Bible study where people gather from all around the world to study the same teaching. For those who want to read and study with other believers, this could be a great place for you too. This particular year, we studied the book Romans in the Bible. In the book, there is scripture related to being judgmental of others and how Paul warns us to not be judgmental.

My mind immediately goes to a famous meme I see circulated on social media, with a picture of Kermit the Frog, saying: *I don't have to walk a mile in your shoes, I can see that you are a train wreck from over here.* I have affectionately excused myself from judging others by acknowledging that all I am doing is simply stating the obvious. People often ask us to consider being kind, not KNOWING what they are "going through," and that we can't be judgmental if we don't know what the exact experience is they are having. I have never lost a parent to death, so I don't know that feeling. I have never broken an arm, so I don't KNOW that feeling. Ultimately, we need to see each other in the same light and mercy that God sees us.

The sympathy we receive from others who know what the challenge or experience is, makes the process of grief or loss validating. What is profound in all of this, is that we are given specific instructions on what to do and what not to do, and still be able to do the things we should not do and, guess what, it's okay. It's not ideal but it's okay. And whether or not it's the result of stupidity or ignorance, the point is we are all walking this same path, trying to see the relevance in all of it. There are things we do that are our activities of daily life and then there are these things we can do that matter more. Don't get caught up in evaluating what is right or wrong in others' lives. Do YOU. Walk your own lane. Look to others who are doing it well. Study them. Study God's word. Read books. Read books and glean from others and use it as an opportunity to grow more efficient at figuring it all out, what it means to live a life of significance. **We aren't here to survive. We are here to thrive**.

We don't have to wonder what to do—it's all written what to do and what not to do. The Ten Commandments are pretty clear as far as basic guidelines go. For the will of God for various decisions we need to make of what to do at crossroads or big decisions we face, we seek God and his confirmation to receive new circumstances or to pay attention to the closing doors. Daily prayer and seeking God's petition of what He wants us to do daily makes this life so much more peaceful.

Our Only Sure Bet

I live in a state where gambling is legal. Prostitution is some of the highest in the nation. You can get a divorce before you can say the word. There may or may not be a bit of a spiritual challenge in our area of Northern Nevada, but it's absolutely beautiful here. We live less than thirty minutes from the Jewel of the Sierra, Lake Tahoe. I remember years ago my husband and I contemplated moving to Idaho. They said it's just like Northern Nevada as far as climate, having all four seasons, but without the gambling, prostitution, and divorce. We were raising a family and I absolutely hated that my boys could see billboards that demoralized women. Remember, I like change and that sounded like a fun move and made sense to minimize what our boys were exposed to. Then I realized that I have access more to what they are exposed to than what they would see on a billboard when getting groceries, driving to church, or sports activities. I had influence on what I could show them;

what is pure, what is lovely, what is excellent and praiseworthy in my broken, sinful, just-doing-the-best-I-can sort of way.

I like change, but I also like sure bets. I like odds that are "ever in my favor." It makes us feel good to have confidence in the outcome. But really, it's total arrogance to believe we have confidence in anything but God. He is our constant. He is all-knowing. He is the one thing we can put our faith, our hope, and our confidence in. Just when we think we have it all figured out and sailing smooth, there are plot twists, forks in the roads, and sometimes what feels like a circumstance we can never come out of.

About ten years ago we purchased a home that was a fixer upper. It was the first home we had that had an acre of land. Our economy was thriving, and I was in real estate at the time, so it was busy. A lot of homes were being bought and sold and home prices were at an all time high. This home needed some work. It was outdated and we needed to make it ours. It was our intention with the size of land we had to be able to allow my parents to build a small home on the property so we could care for them as they aged. We spent a lot of time working on this place, a place to raise our family, a place for memories, and a place for our parents. We met a lot of opposition from people and circumstances outside of our control. While we will never get that time back, we learned a lot of life lessons. There were things we could have seen that we didn't. There was opposition we faced that we hadn't expected.

It's okay to make decisions that don't go as we plan. It's okay to have life lessons that are hard. It was one of the darker times in our lives as we spent time on things that didn't end up going the way we had desired and we did things that in hindsight we won't do again.

We never arrive. We never have it all figured out. Life lessons are valuable, and we can help others possibly avoid some mistakes we made in those dark times of our lives by being vulnerable and sharing our experiences. If I had to go through pain at that capacity so that I could have compassion to never have someone else encounter what we did, I would do it again in a heartbeat. It's okay to go through hard times and we should expect them. It's what we do with what we learn and experience that matters. It's who we seek as our refuge in this process that matters. God allows difficult circumstances, people and situations in our lives to happen and we have a choice to draw closer to Him or retreat. One produces fruit and one produces resentment.

The Truth Hurts

Words from others are powerful. Sometimes when people speak truth into our lives it hurts. It hurts even more if it's true. If someone speaks truth to us and it's actually a lie, we don't need to feel bad. When we lay our head on the pillow at night, we know what our truth is. Sometimes we can be blinded though, by the truth in our lives and we may be in denial, unwilling to accept what is true.

I remember seeking counsel one time from a pastor who is also a licensed therapist. We were discussing hurtful and false things that were being said about me. He explained that it wasn't really truth. It was someone else's perception of the truth about me, but wasn't necessarily true. He proposed the idea that we can only be offended by what we are actually guilty of. There is no need to worry about what others say about us when it's not true. You know your own truth and that is what matters.

We can also pray for God to show us areas of our life that we think we know to be true, but really aren't; exposing them in a way we can repent and seek forgiveness for any wrongdoing. It's okay to make mistakes. We aren't perfect, so why are we trying to be? We are all a work in progress. We are works that move forward. We are works that are created with purpose, for purpose, and on purpose.

We are uniquely woven by God for a plan and for purpose. The sooner we figure that out, the sooner we can be living a life that is meaningful. I don't know that this will be accomplished daily or by the hour, but as often as we can do, say, and be a part of things that matter for this side of eternity, we are fulfilling the amazing works of art that God has planned for us.

Be Good at Making Decisions

You know the end caps of the aisles at the store? They are supposed to catch our eye and attract us to products we might not otherwise see. Trust me, the marketers are brilliant. But one time we were in a store and passed by an end cap and there was a toy that was clearly not part of the product display. The toy was probably entertaining a child while a mother did her shopping at Target that day. *Here, have this and be happy while I get toilet paper and paper towels.* Guilty as charged over here. Clearly with this toy placement, a defining decision was made to display the toy where it didn't belong. Whenever we are in a store and see similar items in places that shouldn't be, we always laugh out loud and say, "A decision was made there."

There are decisions to be made all day, every day. To shower or not? Set an alarm or not? Get food in the house or not? These are life decisions that need to be made and don't have real life altering consequences. Then there are some bigger decisions like finding a different job, a different church, moving into a new city or a new home in the area. God wants to be in the BIG and the little decisions of our lives. He wants to be a part of it all. He wants to be in communication with Him about what He wants for our lives instead of just randomly choosing based on our own intuition or desires. What does God desire for our life?

God is here. He is here right now with you wherever you are: in the valley of despair, or at the mountaintops of joy. It is all by design for Him to be there always. He created us to have relationship with Him. He wants us to spend eternity with Him. He desires fellowship with you wherever you are. I think what hinders us from understanding this is our expectation of what we think we should be experiencing and perhaps believing a certain level of entitlement for how our life should be.

Chapter 9: The Happiest Place on Earth

Those who know me know that I love Disney. Disneyland has always held a special place in my heart. I even remember getting $20 for my birthday one year and It paid for my ticket when my family might not have had the money to go. In fact, Disneyland was where my husband and I went for our honeymoon. We didn't have much money back then and that was a place we could go on a budget and have fun. We had the matching t-shirts and everything!

When our older boys were four and six, we took them for the first time, and we have gone every year since. We never had a lot of money raising a family, but we always had enough in the earlier years to go there for three or four days as our annual vacation. There are extreme enthusiasts of Disney out there and I am even friends with them, but I am not *that* extreme. It's just a place that takes all our cares away. The sights, the sounds, the smells are all nostalgic for me. We don't even go on every ride or visit all the pavilions. We have our own in-park Disney traditions that are very special to us. When Garrett was preparing to leave for the military, all five of us got to go together before he left. Garrett's plan was for the military to be his career, so we knew family vacations would become increasingly limited, so we wanted this one to be extra special.

Toy Story

One morning we did early entry to the California adventure park. Our plan was to go to our favorite ride, Toy Story Mania. When we got there, the ride wasn't up and running yet. We were greeted by an employee, Michael, who assured us it would be up and running soon. We joked around with him in a manner that he later explained was unexpected. He said that typically people feel entitled to have everything go perfect in the happiest place on earth, and when it doesn't, they can be rude or disrespectful. He gestured for us to move over to the side and surprisingly gave us an experience we would never forget. He said that he wanted to reward our kindness and great attitude with an unlimited day-pass to our favorite ride!! *What? Who does that?*

We rode that sucker for hours. At one point after several hours of back to back riding, with arm pump in full swing, he said to us, "You guys are still here?"

"You gave us unlimited pass all day to our favorite ride on a vacation we set out to be a memorable one to cherish for years!" we shouted with glee.

We used that pass to max capacity that day. Michael became a fast-friend. We later became friends with him on Facebook and connected with him in a meaningful way. We have even gone back to the park with Michael and his family since then. Michael doesn't work there anymore because he moved to a job that gave him more time with his family. While we are sad to not have him there anymore, we are grateful for the memorable gift Michael gave our family that day.

We need to have places to go and people to see where we can forget our cares; time to refresh and recharge. Disney is one of those places for us. It's an experience. It's how we perceive it to be. Last summer, we got what I would consider to be an opportunity that most people don't get. It's been a bucket list trip for me for as long as I can remember.

The Disney cruise was always something I wanted to do but never had been able to. We had some friends who know we love Disney and said they were doing it, and asked if we wanted to join them!

We flew to Florida and departed for seven days to the Bahamas Disney style! It was everything I imagined and more. Watching Disney movies poolside—are you kidding me? I love being in the sun and outdoors, and to watch a Disney movie on the big screen, was super special for me. One of their ports is a private Disney island. That stop was one of the best days out of the seven! We snorkeled, ate great food, and ran our toes through the silky sand. It's an experience that holds a lot of great memories, but pales in comparison to a trip that followed a few weeks later.

When the Smoke Clears

After we went to Houston to help with the flood, we were now signed up officially as volunteers with Samaritan's Purse. Once you are in as a volunteer you become part of their database of people who want to serve when the opportunities come up. Once your background check is approved, they provide you with meals and a place to sleep at a host church whenever you are called to help. One of the things we didn't have when we went to Houston was a place to sleep close to where Samaritan's Purse was set up. That made it harder to be effective with the time we were able to give. Having a background check in place helps a lot. We now get text notifications when the need to serve others arises.

There had been several emergencies since we went to Texas, but the timing wasn't right, and we hadn't felt the call to go to any of them. I got a text in early August that Samaritan's Purse had been deployed to Redding, California for the Carr fire, burning in Shasta County. My first thought was, finally, disaster on the West Coast. I was grateful to see this emergency was much closer for us to go and help, since our first one was over sixteen-hundred miles away. As with most people, we had a lot going on at the time with various commitments and the timing didn't seem realistic. If there is one thing I have learned in all my years of choosing to help people, it is that the timing is rarely ideal.

I am not one to watch the news. I used to listen to morning talk television on a fairly regular basis, but it seemed that between elections and the gravity of the landscape for our society as a whole, the news is something my mind has a very hard time processing. Being an empath makes this considerably harder to "shut off" the thoughts of what we expose our eyes and ears to, so I just stopped doing it. Usually when we are cooking dinner there are times when we will have the news on, but only occasionally for me, as it's difficult to process.

One night, Eric was watching the news, reporting on the devastation of the fire in Redding. I commented that I had received a text, that Samaritan's Purse was being deployed there. Without little hesitation, Eric said that we needed to go. We had plans that weekend to be in Utah for a work event for me, and the following week was our 25th anniversary. We decided if it lined up, we would go. We both filled out the application to go serve that night. When we went to Houston, we made the decision to go and an hour later we were on our way. This time, we had a week to plan and prepare.

In the week that followed, there were a lot of obstacles that caused us to doubt whether or not we should go. One of the obstacles was that they had "beds" at the church host home for men, but none for women. One of the things we wished we had the opportunity to do when we went to Houston was to take a team of people with us. The more people who could experience what we were experiencing, the better. So, when we initially started praying and considering going, I posted on social media that if there was anyone who wanted to go, they could join us. We had room for six in our truck. I had a friend that reached out to me on Facebook and said that we were more than welcome to stay with her but that she lived about an hour outside of the fire area. While that wasn't ideal to have a one-hour commute on both ends it was still a possibility.

When we learned that the church host home didn't have a place for us for sure, we phoned our friend and asked her if we could stay. She said everything was all ready to go and please come. She had been hoping and wanted to help with this fire but logistically she could not due to her work schedule. Providing a place for us to sleep gave her a tangible way to have a hand in helping. The hands and feet of Jesus are wide and deep, and come in many shapes and forms. What a blessing it is to know while we don't always have an immediate physical hand in something to help others, there are extensions of the hand like the arm and shoulder and neck that allow the hand to do what it needs to do. For us, it was Rob and Bobbi. They gave us great food and great company and made our place to fall at night and get up for the day extra special.

I had met Bobbi virtually through Facebook about a year earlier as she was someone who was connected to me by means of another friend who was partnered with the supplement company I promote in my practice. What's amazing is to think about the webs of impact that arrive when we say yes to hope. My hope for healing generated healing. The means of that healing helped me to link arms with other people who desired healing. That healing led me to walk out my God-given dream to help those in disaster relief. That decision to move in disaster relief, connected me back to someone who was woven into my life who needed healing. Do you see the impact of what our yes can mean? Saying yes to what God is calling us to do shows others that their mountains are capable of being moved. Those mountains equate opportunities for God to show up in ways that bless our socks right off. He amazes me!

When God calls, He equips and prepares for us. He makes the way. He just needs us to seek His guidance and be willing to go. I promise if you ask, He will show you the way! This experience was very unique on many levels for us. It seemed surreal at times, because here we were to show up and be there for people in a time of despair and the emotions and feelings were very difficult to communicate. When you look into the eyes of people who are doing the same service with you, it's an indescribable experience that makes us feel more complete in our humanity. There are so many things that we do not give thought to on a daily basis about how we live our lives and, more often than not, is lacking true fulfillment that we can become complacent in our humanity. It's in these times where we make a decision to show up for other people in their time of need that truly gives us complete satisfaction of doing what we are created to do and be.

I think back on biblical times when Adam was the only human and how much more complete he felt by having a mate. So much more made sense for the two of them to experience their lives together. This is really what Eric and I have experienced within our decisions to help people in this way. It made me realize when we studied a few years previously the idea of how two are better than one, and how when we do things together that matter, it allows our lives to represent the hands and feet of Jesus. It's us who are truly blessed and grateful for what saying yes to something like this means. It gives a sense of *I was made for THIS.*

You will often hear me say "a few years ago." The fact of the matter is, that could mean two years, or five years, or it could even be eight. Time often blurs as the speed of light does, especially when you throw raising a family in the mix. A few years ago, we were with some friends who I value dearly, and one of them commented on how much he has seen me grow over the years, and how proud he was of me for my spiritual growth and the newfound boldness my life has had. I was incredibly moved by these words. I think it's safe to say it mattered that he felt compelled to edify me with his words. It validated a lot of things for me, with just a few simple sentences on his behalf. I think it takes a special human being to choose to edify others, to lift them up with words and validate who they are. It's like an immediate charge to the soul for a person whose love language is words of affirmation. I don't know many people, regardless of their love language, who don't value hearing people edify the growth God is creating in their life.

Put me in, Coach

Who we surround ourselves with matters. I don't need the biggest cheering section. I have a lot of my own confidence for who I am in Christ Jesus. I am also still very human and fragile, and it fills my tank to hear things about me that matter. It takes a lot of "guts" to live a life out loud. We are subject to criticism from people who are operating out of fear and lack of self-confidence so much so that when they see other people happy and succeeding, it makes them feel less of a person. *People will love us, or people will hate us, and it has nothing to do with us.*

Months before we went to Houston, our pastor gave a message on this very topic. He talked about this idea of "being put in the game," and how God is wanting to put us in the game of being: intentional, proactive, selfless, and operating a life that matters by being in the game rather than sitting on the sidelines. We have so many people living a life on the sidelines, lacking clarity, purpose, and the confidence they need to go and be present for others. He also referred to the reality that when we live a life that matters, doing things like we have done, it makes other people feel uncomfortable as deep down inside they have this God-given ability to do what we are doing. They know they can, but they don't know how to put one foot in front of the other to do it. My hope is that more people will see that Eric and I do not live a life much different than most. We simply put our radar on for the opportunities to see needs for others and DO THEM. I don't want people to see our lives as a poor reflection on theirs and feel bad. I want them to see our lives and see Jesus and say, "Take me with you."

I don't find it coincidental (because I simply don't believe in coincidences), but I was amazed at how God wove our first two disaster relief projects to be both flood and fire. These are two very real disasters that are close to our heart. Both in Houston and Redding I did a live video when I got there to share our experience and both times I wept during the video. When we are spared from tragedy, we should be grateful. Grateful so much so, that when others are in that tragedy too, we feel compelled to go and be empathetic for people. It's powerful to hold that space of healing for others. The opportunity to say, "I know how this feels, I have felt the same way, and here is how I healed."

That, my friends, is what it means to experience pain for a purpose. Pain to a level that we hold people and embrace them powerfully, use our words of comfort, and the arms of Jesus to wrap around them, so that they can feel as if He is there, because HE IS THERE. *He is there through US.* We just need to show up.

The first home we went to help with in Redding burned down in fifteen minutes. This was a HOT fire. The aftermath was so eerie, as there were homes that were burned to the ground, and standing next to them, homes that looked as if nothing happened that day. At one point we went to a neighborhood and there was a couple standing in front of the debris of a home weeping. We went up to them and asked if this was their home. They said no but that it was their friends' and they had tremendous guilt that their home was still standing unscathed across the street.

It's interesting to hear the dialog that we go through in our minds when we are facing tragedy, like a fire coming our way. It first starts with *prepare,* and you may have to evacuate. Then it can go to *mandatory,* meaning you must get out—it's imminent. One of the homeowners we were talking with that week was really wrestling with the idea that he might be wasting his time with packing everything up when it might not actually get to his home. My immediate thought, from the outside looking in, was what if it took you a month or six months to put it all back? Would it be okay if you had to spend time putting it all back and it was in vain?

We are back to this idea that we don't expect tragedy in our lives. We think it happens to others and never to us! That is a lie. Tragedy is real and it's to be expected. I believe it's the expectations we *don't have—but should have—*that we get disappointed with. I talk to a lot of people in my travels, with work and ministry, with friendships and family, and I am often surprised at the reality that people face when tragedy hits their lives.

We are so taken back by it that we often go into crippling despair that takes us away from what we could be doing that matters. Life matters. We matter. What we do and say matters. When we are living through those tragedies or challenges, ask God to give you the strength, the wisdom, and the peace He wants to give you. It makes it so much more palatable when our perspective is to expect the storms. We get so disappointed in the challenge we miss the opportunity for the message we will receive from it. While feeling dejected, hurt, frustrated are normal responses, we often become so self-focused that it doesn't matter. It's supposed to matter. It's there for a reason.

Ask Him how to turn the mess into your message. If you have ever donated blood, the phlebotomist will tell you to prepare for a quick pinch, but it goes away. For some reason in our minds, because we have been told it's coming, we are okay with it and we process it better. The same goes for LIFE. Expect the tragedy. Expect the illness. Expect the loss of job. Expect to be hurt by friends and family. Expect it because we live in a fallen world. But also remember that we have a Creator who can, and will, see us through. One who will use all our experiences to give others the opportunity to learn and grow, and to show how great our God is. God can be there for us and we can be there for others. Let Him in!

Chapter 10: You Should Hear this Girl Pray

The only explanation I have for what I am about to say is God. I cannot, for any other reason or effort, explain the power of prayer. Prayer is an opportunity for us to have conversation with the almighty Father, Creator of the heavens and the earth. He created us to be in relationship with Him. This relationship requires faith for what is unseen, but the evidence is all around. I have what I would consider to be an active presence on social media. I do enjoy talking to people and being in relationships, but it is slightly not an area of strength. I have to initiate conversation with people in person. So social media is a safe platform for me to be in relationship and communicate with others with the propensity to introversion.

I love encouraging others and sharing things of value. We have so much noise in our social media world that the volume is often deafening. I like giving hope to people in what can be an otherwise dark place at times. It's not uncommon for people to share their hopes, fears, illnesses, or tragedies with me. I value meeting these people and praying for them. I don't like to simply say that I am praying for them. While I logistically can't do this all the time, I value writing out my prayer for them in the comments of their status.

I have been commandeered in various roles because people like to have me pray for them. Communication with God is simply communication with God. He is who He is, and we are who we are. He is God and we are not. He created us and wants to be in communication with us. That sense of who we are, and who He is, becomes very real when we open that dialog with Him, and respond when He is dialoguing with us. I don't consider myself "good" at prayer. I simply find an incredible amount of peace in having the powerful dialog with our Creator.

When we were serving in Redding for the Carr fire, everyone we were working with were total strangers, yet they felt like family. It's amazing what barriers go away when you step out in faith and act in a way that is seeking to be there for other people in need. We spent several days with our team leader, Ted. Ted was clearly called by God to be at this place, in this time. God used him and his leadership skills to lead our team. I don't know if it was hard for him to do, but I'm pretty sure God showed up in his life to lead us. It was his first time leading a team and he did it amazingly well. Ted had come all the way from Maine. That says a lot about how logistics have no bounds when we are called to serve. God works out all the details. He has a wife and family that he sacrificed time with to be there for these people, and God honored that.

A good leader will delegate tasks to people to give them opportunities to grow and lead themselves. When we would huddle as a team before going out to a home site, we would pray together out loud as a group. Then, when we would arrive at the home site, we would pray with the homeowner before we started our project. At the end of our time with each family, we would pray again and give them a Bible. Especially in the instance of fire, people might not think to grab their Bible and maybe they don't even have one. With Samaritan's Purse, they are given a special Bible from Billy Graham. One of the jobs the team leader would delegate was presenting the family with this very special Bible, a Bible that only a person who has lived through this kind of tragedy can receive. It's a fulfilling experience to present each family a book that contains so much hope, despite unfortunate circumstances throughout history.

Another role that the leader will ask volunteers to do is to lead the prayers. I was asked to pray at one point during our week. After we prayed, people were coming up to me with their eyes wide open. They were in awe of the prayer. I never know how to receive this type of edification. The only explanation I have is that my prayers are God-led, His words spoken through me to offer peace and hope for those who are listening.

On our last day before we left for home, there was a young gal named Maddie whom I met when we sifted through some debris together. While we were taking a water break and catching a breath of fresh air, she complimented me on how pretty she thought my eyes were. I am not one who needs a lot of compliments, but it sure does make a girl feel good to receive one of that nature. Our team leader walked up as she was saying that and said, "You should hear this girl pray." I have had what I would consider to be a great life. To have someone edify my ability to communicate with God on behalf of others is was one of my greatest moments thus far.

Happiness is an inside job and it's a choice we make. We have full control over our emotions and responses. Our actions are a choice. The words and tapes we play in our heads are a choice. When I go to Disneyland, I choose that I am going to have a good time because I want to have a good time. Are there rude people there? Yes, absolutely. Are the lines long? You bet. Do I have two legs to stand on in that line? Definitely. It's all how we see things that matter. Even when we wait in the long, ridiculous line at the DMV, we have a butt to sit on or we have legs to stand and hands to keep us occupied on our smart devices with internet access and games while we wait. It's all how we see it that matters. Scripture says that the mouth is an outflowing of our heart, and that our tongues can be full of deadly poison. Our words and our thoughts are so powerful and can be a rudder to steer into the pool of positivity, or to the swamp of negativity.

Chapter 11: What About Bob?

Bob Goff is my hero and a well-known author. Bob is an extraordinary human being—he deserves a whole chapter in my book. He took what some would perceive as an ordinary life and chose to make it extraordinary. I don't see myself as any different than Bob. He has had a unique impact on me because of the way he proposes we live our lives. Actions speak volumes over words.

Bob is a great speaker and author, and his words are powerful for so many. Yet his actions speak even louder than his words. Bob believes that we can show love in a way that exceeds words. We can talk about the love of God all day, but we can show who He is that resonates true impact. He has lived out his life demonstrating God's love in powerful and effective ways. Bob is living a life that I admire. God has given him an incredible heart for people in circumstances that others may see as insurmountable, but Bob does it anyway. Bob is ordinary in that he was born, went to school, got a job, is married, and has a family. We first learned of him at a Thrive conference in California. When I heard him speak, I was immediately drawn to his contagious laugh and the way he told his stories.

After hearing him speak, I hopped on Amazon and bought his first book, *Love Does*. Eric and I thought it would be a great way to spend some time together, reading this book out loud, one chapter and day at a time. The chapters are simple, concise, and provide so much inspiration for us. Eric and I finished *Love Does* on our way home from Houston last summer after helping with the flood. I couldn't even make it through the last few pages without tears streaming down my face. I was clearly moved and inspired by what God is doing through Bob. He made me want to live a life that is after God's own heart, to be broken for what breaks His heart. Bob's actions inspire me in BIG ways. As I read the last few pages, I was terribly sad that our time with Bob through this book was coming to an end.

Bob isn't different than you or me per se. He is who he is, and you and I are who we are; each uniquely woven for greatness, with the ability to demonstrate hope and love beyond what words could ever do. *Just like Bob, we too can be the hands and feet of Jesus in ways that speak to people where they never have to question motives or wonder why you choose to live a life this way.*

Tell everyone you know about Jesus and use as few words as possible. That is the life Bob is living. That's what is inspiring to me. That is what Jesus did. He went to the least and showed the most with his actions. I am on Bob's coattails. I have seen him speak in person twice and have read both of his books. Just last night, I was at a fundraiser that Bob spoke at. We took a picture with him and he gave us a few minutes of his time. In our brief conversation, Eric boldly told Bob that I was writing a book and THE Bob Goff, gave me some great advice.

I will forever cherish the time he took with us. He shared a story about a boy that will be receiving a special surgery, who he talked about in his latest book, *Everybody Always*. His excitement for what God was orchestrating was so contagious. Eric and I also read *Everybody Always* together. We would read and talk about each chapter in a way that was intentionally thought provoking and compelled us to up our game. He challenged us both to see people differently and to think outside the box when it comes to this idea of loving everyone always.

Bob leads a conference several times a year that I have often sworn to attend one day. The conference is affectionately titled *Dream Big*. It's a place where he helps facilitate people learning and doing more of what desires God puts in their hearts to do that matter. I have full faith and confidence that in the right timing, I will attend his conference one day. God weaves the most humorous, yet equally creepy-in-a-fun-sort-of-way little glimpses that He is so real and relevant in our lives. Last spring as I wrapped up my study on the book of Romans for Bible Study Fellowship, I had lunch with our leader, and she invited me into leadership.

We talked a lot about what God had been doing in our lives and where I was feeling called to be. I shared with her that I feel called to teach but hadn't received clarity on what that would be or where. She and I are a lot alike and we had a lot of the same hopes and desires with living our lives in ways that matter. As we left lunch that day, the waitress brought my leftovers in a box with the words Dream Big written in bright yellow ink. My jaw dropped to the floor and I quickly turned it into a gigantic smile knowing our God has a plan and it is good.

Bob's Advice

A few pieces of advice Bob left with me last night that may help you too:

1. Have an immense amount of patience for people.

2. Just throw the ball while stepping closer and closer to people.

3. Don't wait for a plan.

4. See people as who God is turning them into, not who they are.

While I have not described a significant hardship on a grand scale of life experiences for comparison, I do hope that you can see that no matter what we go through, big or small, it all matters. We all process and heal from grief, tragedy, and loss on a variety of levels. There is no right or wrong way to navigate these things. There is hope no matter what the degree is. *We all live in the shell of humanity and we all can choose to move through it with significance and with purpose.* We have been progressing as a society, the pace increasing every day, becoming more technologically advanced in leaps and bounds, yet still incredibly pressed for time. I hear and have used the phrase "busy" like it's a badge of honor.

Distracted Thriving

I heard an acronym for busy once that made me feel like I was using foul language when I used it: *being under Satan's yoke.* Not a badge of honor I want to have. Over the last few years we have become increasingly distracted. In fact, Eric coined the phrase recently when he wrote a blog for our church and the title of the blog was called *Distracted Thriving.* This is an interesting play on words for the distracted ways we succumb to filling our lives with things, experiences, and activities that, in the big scheme of things, don't really matter. *Before you know it, we are so focused on just keeping up that we lose sight on being present and involved with things that have eternal value.* I will be the first to tell you we have fallen victim to this distraction plenty of times in our time together, but we are starting to get a glimpse as we grow in our faith to do more of what matters.

Recently we watched a documentary on Netflix called Minimalism. It is the philosophy of people living with the bare minimum. Having less stuff gave them the ability to see more clearly than when their minds were cluttered with the distractions of all this *stuff.* I was enamored with how simple and uncomplicated this lifestyle looks and I am drawn to it. I feel I have a lot of clutter holding me back from the clarity to do more of what matters.

The more "stuff" we manage, the more time it takes away from having a life of significance. I don't know about you but I want to be better at having more understanding of living in a way that is different from this modern world full of stuff, and create a positive ripple effect that compels people to be more grateful for what we have, and for seeing the good that can come from life's challenges. I love a good comeback story and I am the biggest cheerleader for the underdog, *always.*

Chapter 12: Be Made of Courage

We were made to be courageous. The more courage we exercise, the braver we get. The more courageous we get, the more we are able to see what God can do in and through us. Because I was brave all those years ago to serve in our local church community, the struggles created more space for courage. Because Eric and I chose to be very public with our first two disaster relief experiences, we have had several conversations with others about how inspiring it is to see us living this courageous kind of life. They seem surprised that it's possible. When we step out in faith and have courage, it gives people the ability to have their own courage. We are, in all fairness, the same in our humanity. The ripple effect from our choice to be courageous can, and will, spread. Bob inspired us on many levels and our hope is that we can inspire others who make that choice to live more of a courageous life. There are a whole lot of people hurting in this world. They need each of us to stand beside them in their mess and be Jesus to them. If we knew the outcome was certain, we would see a lot more people living this way. But these choices involve being courageous in uncertainty. This is where God shows up in mighty and profound ways—where the only explanation is God. *I want to live more of a life where the only explanation can be God!*

Most people just want to be seen, heard, and held. There isn't a whole lot of special training that needs to happen for that. Like Bob said, there doesn't need to be a plan. When we plan, God laughs. We make it far more complicated than it needs to be. One small step turns into another step which turns into a leap and a stride, and before you know it, you are off and running to live a life of immeasurable purpose: to help those who are hurting. Ask God to show you who and He will do the rest.

Consistency Breeds Success

Keep at it. Consistency breeds success. When we lack consistency, we are in the process of quitting. Don't give up. Be consistent to what God placed in your heart. Write it out. Tell others about it and watch the beauty unfold. It was likely three years from the time we read *Dream Giver* to when we took our trip to Houston to help with the floods.

You are becoming who you are the more you speak what desires and dreams God puts in your heart. **Spoiler alert: *The things of this world that we strive to grasp at to make us feel complete and accomplished, look very different than the dreams God places in our path*.** I have done a variety of things that make me feel accomplished and worthy of sharing with others, but these pale in comparison to the real desires, God's desires in our hearts.

I find it ironic that each time we chose to walk out in faith towards a disaster relief project, a few weeks prior to each trip we were on some sort of bucket list vacation. I also find it interesting both disaster relief trips and these bucket list vacations were also in our anniversary month. You see, so many times we try to piece together things of value as the world sees it *when God is trying to piece together things of value as He sees it*. We learn and we grow. Doing things that matter have a cost. They cost us our control that we like to have. They cost us comfort that makes us feel safe. They cost us the loss of our self-seeking life in exchange for a selfless one, so that others may regain their hope. Shock and awe are the two words that come to mind when we show up for other people. It's incredibly humbling to make a choice to show up and be there for people. *It's a series of fortunate events that will fill spaces in your soul that no dream vacation can ever fill*. It's a place where God shows up in a way that makes you experience Him in ways you could never imagine. *It's a way for us to become who really we are.*

The People

One thing that made our experience in Redding almost indescribable were the people themselves. Something miraculous happens when you show up for those who have lost everything with other volunteers who are there to help too. One of our team leaders was from Maine, someone else from Hawaii, hundreds of locals rallied for their community.

It made me question how often I show up for my own community, even when there *isn't* a disaster. Every day, there are people struggling in our own communities, who simply want to be heard, held, and hugged. We don't need a natural disaster to experience people who are hurting. These people are all around us every day and sometimes those people are us. If we don't allow people that God is using to be there for us, how do those people get the opportunity for God to use them? Allow people in. It matters. Is it possible that God allows things in our lives so that we need others and so that others can utilize what God is placing in their heart to be there for you in yours?

Last week we were at a fundraiser Bob Goff was speaking at. The funds were going towards impoverished kids in our community, who otherwise wouldn't know who Jesus is. This organization makes a path for these kids to be shown who Jesus is. When I am participating in this type of opportunity to bring awareness, I find myself seeking God and asking if this is an area I could be used in. I am drawn to a lot of things that need attention, but I can quickly spread myself too thin. I want to save as many people as I can. Our world is broken. There are devastated people all around us. When we show up in our brokenness and we help fill in the cracks of others, that act of selflessness is the making of our oneness and wholeness with God. Never consider what you have to offer others as insignificant. There will always be people out there who need whatever you can give.

The Adventure with Bessie

One of Eric's dreams has been to restore cars for fun. A few months ago, he popped his head in my office at about 7:30 in the evening while I was on a conference call and mouthed the words, "I'm flying to Long Beach, California in the morning to buy a 1964 Chevy Suburban."

At 10:09, as we settled into bed, I asked him to tell me more about this plan of his, not considering that he was serious. About 80% of what comes out of Eric is rhetoric for comic relief. As he continued to share his plan, I realized he actually purchased airfare and was indeed flying out first thing in the morning. The more I heard him talk about this vehicle he was in pursuit of and how badly he wanted it, the more I wanted to go!

"Take me with you on this adventure!" I said. He quickly admonished my desire and said that it would be hot, bumpy, uncomfortable, and that he was not even entirely sure if we would make it the five-hundred-mile drive home. I immediately calmed his fear, grabbed my phone and made my air reservation. We were going on an adventure and the only thing that matters is that we have each other!

Let it be known that car restorations are not my thing. However, being with Eric and being adventurous with my best friend is. It is all how we perceive it and what we want it to be. Call it an adventure and so shall it be. Call it scary and so shall it be. When we arrived in Long Beach there was a very nice man in his early 30s named Jason waiting to pick us up at the airport. We were pleasantly surprised that he didn't appear to be a serial killer, even though his name was Jason, and were confident he wasn't going to chop us up and put us in the back of his car.

We took this classic beauty for a drive and found it to be pretty much what the ad had said. Jason said he was confident it would make the five-hundred-mile drive home, so we went to the bank and got him some cash. We were on our way home within less than 24 hours of me booking my flight. Eric was a bit nervous about whether or not we would make it home in this beauty we now affectionately refer to as Bessie. We stopped at a Walmart and got duct tape, screwdrivers, paper towels, oil and antifreeze, just in case, and we kept moving forward. Happy to say we survived. Our girl Bessie got us home safe and sound.

Sometimes we don't have a plan and that is okay. God wants us to be adventurous with Him. He doesn't want us to have it all mapped out. He wants for us to trust Him and the process of being bold, brave, and confident in who He is and what His plans are for us in the adventures of life. Sometimes we break down and the tow truck and emergency gas cans come in handy. Sometimes He fills our tanks with antifreeze (also known as *don't panic, I got this* fluid) and sometimes He is there to re-fuel or jumpstart the process when it doesn't go as planned.

We trust and He drives. He is our co-pilot and there is so much beauty in the adventure of not knowing how it will all go! It's all how we perceive it. Prepare mentally and expect bumps in the road for all of it, both the mundane and the extraordinary. He wants to use us as His vessels in it all. We also don't get to pick and choose what parts of life we are content with and grateful for. We have to be content with every aspect. We can't say we embrace the good times, but not the bad. We can't expect that it's always going to go as we plan and that is ok. **Be grateful for all of it.** It's amazing how our perspective changes when we are grateful for it ALL.

Chapter 13: Power in Prayer

After our miscarriage in 2000, we decided that it was still God's plan for us to have another son or daughter. After you experience loss of life, you no longer care what the sex is of the gift God gives you. You receive this life as His, and we trust the One who made us to make that choice. We conceived our next baby Caleb less than 60 days from our previous loss. Fear set in fast at the reality of what may come with this pregnancy and the potential to have to navigate another sad circumstance. Life is precious and all too often we take it for granted. I took for granted the baby prior to this one was a sure bet of life. There is nothing sure except God's unfailing love and faithfulness.

As mentioned earlier in the book, one of the hardest parts of my miscarriage was telling people. I didn't like repeating the sad story to everyone around me. I held too much guilt, thinking I had not done all the right things. I didn't like reliving that pain with each new conversation. I didn't want to tell anyone we were expecting another baby. With each passing day knowing we were expecting another baby, fear of the unknown kept taking away our ability to have people petition the Lord on our behalf, the name of Jesus. There is power in His name. The more people saying His name, the more peace we have despite the outcome. Prayer changes us. I'm honored to pray on others' behalf, and I appreciate when people pray for me.

Layers of Bravery

I believe bravery is matured in layers. Every time we step out and operate out of bravery in a vulnerable way, knowing *we* are not in control and that the Almighty God *is*, He gives us the gift of bravery. The more we seek to be in commune with others in prayer, the more we grow in peace. This peace transcends all understanding and that's the sweet spot God wants us in. He doesn't desire us to be stagnant, our growth stunted. He wants us thriving, not barely surviving.

When we did finally share the news of another baby on the way with our family, there was so much peace. We decided that we didn't want to bear the potential of the unknown on our own and how much we wanted our friends and family to rally for us in prayer. Partnership is powerful and so is prayer. The peace that followed the decision to seek the prayers of our friends and family that no matter what the outcome was, we appreciated their going on our behalf to our Heavenly Father and they sought His peace for us all. What a relief it was to let it go and seek communal prayer.

One time I was flying into our hometown from a business trip. It's historically windy landing into Northern Nevada even when the weather is fine. We were experiencing a wind that I've never experienced before and by the looks on the faces of my fellow passengers, neither had they. I had Wi-Fi on my phone and hopped on social media asking for prayers from my fellow prayer warriors to lift up our flight, our pilots, and our level of peace God was desiring us to have—and it was so.

Peace isn't changing the outcome, it's changing our ability to trust God through the fire and the storm. He is always there and wants to give us His peace. It's okay to be in a position of need with others. We were not designed to be self-reliant. We are designed to be in communion with one another and with our Creator. We should believe and operate out of that belief. The more people we have believing that we are all the same, that we all have the same basic needs, that we all desire to be to be loved and known, the more we take down the walls of pride: the more we become one in our humanity.

Belief at the Root Level

Believe you are ordinary, and so shall it be. Believe you are extraordinary, and so shall it be. There is no doubt we are all wired in our humanity the same way. It is God who uses us for the extraordinary. He desires to be the extra in our ordinary. There are plenty of examples of this in the Bible, stories of ordinary people who God used to do extraordinary things, things that mattered. If our root system is such that we lack belief in who God created us to be, the weaker our foundation is. Roots matter. We grow our roots deep when we are rooted in God's word, fellowship with other believers, and in our personal relationship with our Creator. The roots are the source of life. A tree cannot bear fruit without the roots. The roots are paramount for the trunk and the branches to grow.

Mary was a thirteen-year-old virgin who delivered to us the savior of the world. He used David, a small guy to defeat a giant. He used Noah to save the remnants before the flood. Mary, David, and Noah are you and me. We share the same Creator who created each of us for purpose and to live a life that matters. We have the power of prayer to keep us connected. What you believe is what you will experience.

Lie or truth: I am capable.

Lie or truth: I am worthy.

Lie or truth: I am His.

Choose YOUR words and choose your lie. Change your lie and change your life.

Our prayer for one another lightens the burden we feel. Have you ever moved? Moving is a daunting task. Not only have we moved a lot, we have helped people move. In fact, I have always said that we find out who our friends are when we move. Be that guy. Be that girl who shows up on moving day. It's an amazing thing to have witnessed the look on homeowners' faces when the posse of Samaritan's Purse volunteers roll up in our rented U-Haul vans and trucks. It's like watching a huge weight being lifted off their shoulders. Their circumstances don't change, but the level of peace they have does. These are the moments I thank God I am alive and well enough to be that person who shows up for other people in their pain.

A New Way of Adjusting

People never get their life back after a tragedy. They just find a new way of adjusting to the change in the landscape they live in. We desire to be validated. We desire to be loved. We desire that people who otherwise shouldn't care, do. It's not what we say we are going to do; it's actually showing up and doing it that matters. Prayer for those suffering is extremely important, but so is showing up and taking action.

Community gives hope to humanity. Hop on to social media for 10 minutes, and before you know it, you are scrolling faster and faster passing all the muck and mire. Are we really that depraved? Is our world really that dark? Perhaps, it's even darker than that. Still, we are called to be that light in the darkness. The more we show up and demonstrate to people the best of humanity, the more people can see themselves as wanting to be a part of an effort to rise above the ashes and to say, "I am sorry you are hurting. Let me help you by lightening your load."

When we selflessly show up for others, God fills in the cracks of brokenness in a situation. He uses us not on our merit or strengths, but on His merit and His strength.

What we are called to do is say "yes" when He calls.

We lay our head on the pillow each night having said to Him, "Lord, use me today as you see fit. Give me the strength and courage to be a vessel of your love." Some days it's in the ordinary and some days it's going to be extraordinary. Believe you can be used, and you will. Desire to be used and offer yourself up to be used, and God will use you. How much easier could it be? If it were effortless it would be of little value. It will be messy, but, when you show up for others in their mess, it will be worth it!

It's equally important to let other people show up for you in your mess. Give yourself permission. It's okay to show up for what God puts on you. You get a "Yes" from God, and you go.

Chapter 14: The Commodity of Time

Recently I was having a conversation with my son's mother-in-law. We were talking about the cost of labor for renovating her backyard. I commented that there are 40 hours we work a week and she asked what are we left with? She said, "We all start with 168 hours a week. 40 hours for a job, 56 hours for sleep, and that leaves us with 72 hours in a week. 72 divided by 7 days a week is 10 hours a day." What are we doing with those 10 hours a day? That's more hours per day than we sleep or are at work! Indeed, math is black and white. When we claim we don't have time to do what matters, we don't lack of time, we lack of priority. When push comes to shove, we choose how we spend our time. *Time is that precious commodity we spend that often leaves us bankrupt, borrowing from Peter to pay Paul when we have it all along.* **We choose** how we spend it!

I am spending my time today on this keyboard, even though I have a gazillion other things to do. I believe what is written here is God-inspired, God-breathed. Regardless of whether anyone else will ever find it valuable, this is what obedience looks like when God puts things in your heart to do. It's not always about the end result, **it's about the process of obedience**. Sometimes we will never know the true fruit of what our "yes" will bear, but that isn't our role. Our role is in the yes and in the Amen. We either say yes and put other tasks off for a time, or we say no. Some days the scale is a little grander than others and we get in our car and drive to help someone 300 miles away, or sometimes we take a meal to a friend who just lost a loved one. *Jesus shows up for others through us.*

This is His plan all along. Nothing we do or don't do is catching Him by surprise. His desire is that we figure it out sooner rather than later. That is my hope too. I value trying to reach out and help someone figure out the more profound way sooner rather than later. This life is profound. You matter. What you do in and with this side of eternity matters. The more you move in what matters, the braver you get for doing more of that. That is what Jesus is saying with each yes He gives us that we accept. Do more of that and He will show you the way.

Are We There Yet?

I have found myself in the process of writing this "book" that I keep looking at my word count. Am I there yet? Am I there yet? Am I supposed to focus on the process or am I supposed to focus on the purpose? Have you ever been in a situation that was painfully long? Maybe it was something as mundane as the dreaded department of motor vehicles or perhaps a class of some sort that is taking an eternity. When I am at church on Sunday, a common place people look is at the clock and ask, "is it over yet?" This is sad to me, to think that we fail to miss the point of the purpose in the process.

I love going to church. I enjoy the people. I enjoy the message of encouragement and correction. I never watch the clock. My mindset is that I am here to learn and excited to be here. Sometimes we get into these various life circumstances and we watch the clock as if each passing stroke of the minute hand is making it go quicker. Newsflash: watching the clock doesn't make it go any quicker. Sometimes we fail to see the beauty in time allotted in what God has for us, because we are busy waiting and watching for it to be over. What if we stopped watching and wishing for the end, and embraced the time frame itself? The time frame for whatever it is, is by design. **We can't be distracted by comparison when we are captivated by purpose.**

Growth Through Challenge

There is growth that needs to happen in each of us in these challenges. Expect the challenge. Expect the growth process that more often than not is painful. The sooner we get the lesson, the sooner we can grow forward. We can't get the lesson when we are staring at the clock wishing for it to be over. All too often we are anticipating the end when, until we understand what is in the middle, the hands of the clock will move slower and slower. We must stop trying to control the middle and seek the growth that is supposed to happen while we wait. Looking for the light at the end of the tunnel helps our minds process that hope is on the horizon. Hope is always on the horizon when our perspective is on the giver of hope, rather than the hope itself. He gives us the ability to persevere in the time frame needed when our focus remains on Him.

Seek Him in whatever is being allowed in your season right now and release your desire to try and fix the outcome. Our growth in the process is the point to it all. We race to "do" so much in life. We run around trying to check all the boxes we have been conditioned by our society to check, while we miss the point of it all. We are not human doings, we are human BE-ings. Be You. Be brave. Be Patient. **Be submissive to the people, the process, and the point of it all. Are we Here yet**? Be here, where God has you, and trust the purpose of the process.

Navigating Fear

About a year ago I decided to join a local gym. I have never been wild about the idea of belonging to a gym, as I could see myself making excuses even before the gym membership was solidified. I had predetermined I would not be committed. They say you should find something you absolutely love doing, so you are less likely to make excuses for why you don't go. It should also be in close proximity to your home or office, so that the distance isn't an issue. So, find something you love, make sure it's close by and go for it! There are a lot of people that come to this gym whose work is right across the street. It's convenient and they make it happen. There have been different aspects about this particular gym, as far as the classes offered, that have intimidated the heck out of me. With one of them, simply the fear of the unknown scared me. One day I decided in order for me to help other people up their game with their fitness level, (since I am a health coach and all), was to overcome my fear of this class.

Fear is not false evidence appearing real. Fear is the expectation of pain. Fear is being uncertain of an outcome. I expected to have this particular class "pain me" and so I operated out of that fear. But guess what? I faced my fear and the expectation of pain and did it anyway! Was it hard? Absolutely. Was is worth it? Absolutely! Not just because I showed myself I what was capable of, but for having the ability to overcome my fears and show other people that it *is* possible.

Sometimes God allows us to go through difficult times, to show other people that He can move their mountain too. This is why it is so powerful for us to live life as God created us to be in BIG ways; to go through the trials and come out the other side with incredible purpose, no matter how hard the trial. So many good things come when we choose to do tough things, to face our fears and expectations of pain, and do it anyway! We CAN do hard things and they are so worth it.

This life is not simple. It's not always easy. Easy things generally are tacky. One good step turns into another bold move. Being bold generates courage. Not being okay with mediocrity creates a ripple effect. We are created for more than we could ever imagine.

What are the steps for living this kind of purpose-filled life? How do you eat an elephant? One bite at a time. Start small and work your way forward. Progress creates history and history dictates the future. Do more of that. **The more we serve the clearer the mission field gets.**

When we were new to our church, there were some common questions that would come up when trying to get to know people. Are you married? How long? Do you have kids? What are their ages? Usually that is the breaking point where shame sets in and I lose sight of the rest of the conversation. Saying out loud how long we have been married and the ages of our kids brings about an incredible amount of shame—not the feel-good conversation of the year for me. I am remorseful that I didn't choose God's best plan for me, and it's something I have to live with. Or do I? Do I have to live with it, our can I live without it?

The math never changes, but what I do with it can. Here is where trajectory takes place. Here is where purpose comes in. Some of the leaders in our church asked me to share our story from the pulpit on a Sunday. I decided that if I didn't want someone else to make the same choices I made, I should share the choices I made. When Eric and I first met, our relationship went immediately into the fast lane. We moved in together as a financial strategy. We got engaged after two short months of being together. Somehow deep down I knew he was the one for me, but I didn't trust God enough to allow for His timing rather than ours. I didn't trust Him enough to let it be His best plan for our life by having a pure relationship. After moving in with each other, despite family counsel that it wasn't a good idea, I started losing the diamonds from my engagement ring. One by one they fell out with each passing day. We began to struggle with our relationship. Playing house when we weren't married left much opportunity to miss out on God's best for our lives.

There clearly is a way to seek God in the biggest decisions for our lives and we were leaving that key component out. We knew the answer. We had our fingers plugging our ears. *Its okay God, we got this.* Before we knew it, we were separated and I found myself expecting our first baby, feeling completely alone. Our God is a God of order and when we put Him at the forefront of our decisions and seek His way, the dominos stand erect. When we do it our way, lacking trust and guidance, those dominos fall down. In sharing our story, there were a lot of people who found they could relate, not only to the relationship decisions we had made, but also the complete lack of trust in God for His best plan for our lives. When we trust Him, we trust all of His ways and timing.

It turns out when you retire, all of your friends and family will ask you to help do stuff for them. Help me move. Fix my car. Build this. Lead that. It has come in a lot of shapes and forms in the last year and a half. Some of them, Eric has enjoyed doing as they are things he has a natural propensity for. He also enjoys a good challenge. Some of those things have been outside his wheelhouse and he has still figured out a way to do it. We often joke about how he should go back to work so he can get some rest. Most days he climbs in bed at night equally, if not more exhausted, than when he was working. What doesn't weigh as heavy on his heart though, is the depravity of our society.

Having been in law enforcement for twenty-five years, he dealt with the worst of our society on a daily basis; working with people who failed to see what their true purpose was in life. They made one bad decision after another, with far-reaching consequences. Often for law enforcement officers, the only source of their hope from the daily grind comes from an occasional award for doing their job that resulted in a life being saved. We have to have those glimpses of light at the end of our tunnel. For him, those glimpses were few and far between in the workforce.

We live our lives based on the seasons: spring and summer, fall and winter. Our lives are seasonal too. What is important is that we see the season for what it is. Then we ask God to give us the strength to weather our God-given opportunities for new perspectives, new scenery, and new ways for us to be used as the vessels of God.

Chapter 15: Shrink out the Bad by Adding in the Good

In the nutrition wellness world that I live in, I help others find more peace and happiness with their physical bodies. We often talk about this idea of how we can crowd out the bad foods by adding in more of the good foods. The more good food we put in our bodies, the more our bodies want good food. Eat garbage and the body wants more garbage. It's a cycle not many can actually visualize breaking free from.

Food is comforting to us, satisfying. Only the stuff that isn't ideal fades quickly and leaves us with a false sense of nourishment. When I went to school, they taught us how to overcome objections people will have and hurdles they will face by overcoming them ourselves first. This way we can identify with where people are at in their struggle, and share that we know how they feel, and how we overcame what they are facing. We hold that space of healing for them, then step aside so they can move into that same space of overcoming. When we keep saying yes to the right things, more optimal things, our bodies will want those things as well.

The same goes for our stewardship of the time, talent and abilities we have been given on this side of eternity. We otherwise miss out on a lot of important things in life when we are indecisive with our yes. Say yes and follow through. It builds character. It makes us reliable. As we keep showing up, our commitments become unshakable. We all have this deep-rooted, God-given desire to *belong*; to be in fellowship with other people and to be known on an intimate level, so that we learn what makes their hearts beat and they can learn what makes ours beat. Yes, it's risky to put ourselves out there and share, as we fear people won't encourage or edify us in that decision to share that piece of what makes us unique, and that is okay. The process of sharing who we are isn't to please people; it's to share what makes you, YOU. We are here to be KNOWN. You are KNOWN by the One who made you. The more you have confidence in the ONE who KNOWS you most, the more you will feel empowered to celebrate who made you.

We live in such a fast-paced society. It seems like the more technologically advanced we get, the more strapped for time we are. True relationships end up taking a back seat. We become complacent in this vital role we have in our humanity, and that is the idea of sharing our lives with each other in ways that matter. We must be intentional with the act of being KNOWN, and in desiring to learn more about others in ways that matter.

To be known is a wonderful feeling. This idea that we open ourselves to a place of being vulnerable enough to let people into the real us is an incredibly powerful place to be. We all struggle. We are all living in a broken world where sometimes the thought of even putting our feet on the floor to get out of bed and go face that world is daunting. Eventually though, we have to get out there and be who God created us to be. To share His love and His light in a world that often leaves us feeling bankrupt.

We have choices for how we handle this side of eternity. Let us choose to let people in our lives, and be the ones to help others who might not have it all figured out yet. We don't have to know it all. We just have to know enough. Invite people to come to a place where they can feel valued, loved, and truly known.

What can you share with your circle that matters? What can they learn about you that you can share with them in an authentic and vulnerable way that they will love to learn about you? What can you do to receive people in a way that gives them a sense of safety, a sense that you will be there for them in the future? Look for people who share your values, can edify you, and can admit they are on the same path with you. Community is powerful. Maybe you love hip-hop music? Maybe there is a particular movie genre that you enjoy? Perhaps you have a heart for aging adults? Whatever it is, seek out people who can help you be known, and you can know them too. Being known and knowing others matters. You matter. They matter. Life on this side of eternity matters.

Time Management

I know what you are thinking. You are already strapped for time, right? How do you begin to even think about what this kind of life looks like when you already have barely enough time to breathe some days? Today is one of those days for me. Rushing from appointment to appointment, and project to project.

We all have the same twenty-four hours in a day. We have a time priority problem. Certain things just aren't important enough to be penciled in as a priority yet. Yesterday morning when I was doing some writing, I looked at my clock and realized I hadn't managed my time that morning as well. The time for a shower before church escaped me. It became a dry shampoo, extra deodorant, and shower later kind of day. I was conflicted in that moment as I was also feeling compelled to write. A message was coming to me. I began to panic and for a split second feared that if I didn't keep writing, I would forget where I was with my train of thought, but I also knew that I needed to be at church that morning.

While it's important that I write as God leads me to, it's also important to me to be in regular fellowship with other like-minded people. Fear gripped harder and I panicked about having to make a decision to keep writing as I felt compelled by God to do, versus the importance of being in church with my family. It wasn't long before I realized that if God was truly inspiring me, I was not in control. If I wasn't able to put these thoughts put to paper now, he would give them to me later as well.

It's kind of like looking for a cure before getting a diagnosis. We try and find the answers when the answers are there all along. Trust the one who made you, and trust that if He has led you to something, He can lead you through to completion. God desires to be in on every aspect of your life. He wants all of us, every part of us, to seek Him and His guidance, His direction, His peace, and clarity. He desires to help us bring our God-given dreams to fruition. Six weeks ago, I didn't know I would have a desire write a book, or that God had a plan for me to do so. The next step is to finish and pray about where and how He wants it distributed. Maybe there is just one reader it needs to go to, or maybe ten. Maybe it's just for me to be obedient, to answer His call to write down all of the amazing ways God has shown up in my life, to show you He wants to show up in yours too.

Passing the Baton

We are called to lead people in the direction of finding purpose in their pain. About twenty years ago, I began attending Bible study. My very first discussion group leader was a lady by the name of Jean. She reminded me of my grandma Mary. She had an incredible heart and I just loved her. She commanded such wisdom! I knew I wanted to listen to whatever she had to say.

I have always admired selfless people. People who put others' needs before their own. Jean taught me that, showing me the value of sacrificing my time. Jean inspired me that one day I, too, could lead other women. I began to see that sacrifice to serve others would be worth the time spent, and that God would equip me if I was called to have such a role. I valued connecting with the other women in my group who were all doing "life" with me, and that we all wanted to learn how to do it well by studying God's word. It resonated with me that we have to do more of what matters.

Shortly after of being in Jean's group, I was invited into leadership for Bible Study Fellowship. I prayed about it and I felt confident that if God was equipping me, I would have what I needed to fulfill a leadership role. Jean showed me that God had equipped her and because she showed me how, it gave me the confidence to do the same. I was in leadership with Bible Study Fellowship for four years, until I had our youngest son Caleb. When he was born, I took some time off to get a better handle on my new role to being a mom to three.

I never anticipated being away from Bible study so long. In sixteen years, it never occurred to me to go back to Bible study, until two years ago when I had lunch with a friend from church. When we met for lunch she was running late and said she was coming from the same Bible study organization I had been part of all those years ago. As we chatted about where she had been, I quietly wondered to myself why in the world had I let sixteen years go by without going back to Bible Study Fellowship? It was a significant time in my life. I grew a lot. I wondered why it had not even come up on my radar. I was immediately compelled to be a part of this group again, and the following week I was back, once again in fellowship with another group of amazing women.

The following year, I attended again and was invited back into leadership. This is my first year back in leadership. I am so amazed at God's perfect timing and His calling of those He equips. I knew this year was going to be special when I looked at my roster of group participants to see that Jean, my former and very first leader, was placed into my group. She is now in her early 90s. What an honor it was to see her name on my roster. We have been back at our study for a few weeks now and, sadly, Jean has been unable to attend so far this year due to declining health. I have had the opportunity to speak with her and let her know what a blessing it was to even see her name on my roster, as she was one who showed me how God equips those He calls. She inspired me that I, too, could have a role in which I would guide women to walk with God by studying His word.

As I drove home from Bible study today, God showed me that Jean has passed on the baton. She has run her race and I am now the next carrier of what God can do in and through us when we say yes to our callings. Keep saying yes to what God calls you to do. It's not always easy, but it will certainly be worth it.

It fills a space in the heart with a tremendous amount of peace to know what it means to be doing more of what matters. There is always sacrifice involved and that is the chasm God fills, showing us what He created us to do. There are things that we do in this life to fill gaps that don't hold a whole lot of value or meaning, and there are things we do that may seem odd, where people question the selfless nature of the role we play. The world won't always understand what it is, or what it means to live a life that not only brings us true gratification, but a unique understanding of what it means to walk out a life of significance.

Time is a commodity we don't get back. It's important that we spend it well: with people and in ways that matter in the grand scheme of this life. I am forever grateful to Jean for showing me what it means to demonstrate a life of sacrifice; for doing more of what can bring glory to God; and to help someone else to see what we can say and do that will have a ripple effect on the lives of others.

Who are you holding the baton for? What can you do that matters? How can you show others how easily we can say *yes*? How can you demonstrate that God provides us with the ability to do it? How can you show that anyone can have a positive ripple effect on others' lives? Money, experiences, and opportunities will fade. There is so much more to this life than we can ever imagine!

Put Fear in its Place

I have said it before: I feel this idea of fear is gripping our society in profound ways. The simplest explanation for fear is the expectation of pain, and being uncertain of the outcome. In our humanity we don't like to experience pain and whatever it is that we are facing, contemplating, or avoiding is often the result of false expectations. A valid fear is that if we touch a hot stove, we can expect to feel the pain of a burn. That's not a fear we want to face and do it anyway. Speaking in public is one of the most common fears people have. I have had to overcome a lot of fears in my forty-six years, including speaking in public. One of my fears in public speaking is that I would say something and not communicate it well enough for people to understand—the fear of being misunderstood.

In the wellness industry, we as thought leaders often face criticism for having an agenda to help others that generates revenue. Is it not okay to help people and generate income? That is what most industry is, barring non-for-profit organizations, and even those leaders need to pencil in an income somewhere.

Fears can be valid, but that doesn't mean they aren't something we cannot overcome. We can embrace being bold, brave, and unapologetic for what we have to offer this world. There are people out there that could benefit from what we have to say or do. The impact is profound. Remember, inmates don't like to see other inmates escape. There will always be people who operate out of fear and trepidation that being confident in who we are makes others feel uncomfortable when they don't understand their own true purpose. It's not a reflection on us. It is a direct reflection on who *they* are, their own lack of confidence.

Some people fear change because they fear the potential for the outcome to not be in their favor. Fear of making mistakes is paralyzing. I believe my love for change has strengthened me, as with each passing choice to experience change has led to growth. It's how we process it and what we call it that generates the most growth.

Eric was in a training session at work, where the question was posed to the group: *Who was the greatest teacher of all time?* Being in this particular setting hadn't afforded him the opportunity to consider what the ultimate answer would be. There were a lot of responses, but the correct answer the instructor gave was *Jesus Christ.* Eric was devastated that he hadn't considered that when the answer was given. He agreed, regrettably, that his answer was incorrect. God is the God of second chances and later in his career, Eric was given another opportunity to answer this same question. He boldly stood up and announced with utter joy, "Jesus Christ!"

Standing in His Love

I have made mistakes throughout life. However, there are no bad experiences or outcomes, as they are all something we can learn and grow from. Sometimes we face consequences that aren't ideal. That doesn't mean we hang them up on the "I can't learn from this rack." Our oldest son Jared is very calculating. Few conversations are had with him where math calculations, percentages, or dividends aren't discussed. He loves working through statistics and calculations. I do not. He carefully considers his decisions, and typically the odds are in his favor if he is choosing to do something! I love that about him.

Sometimes, though, we need to lean more into our faith, rather than our calculations. God calls us to do, say, and experience things where the math isn't always justified and where the outcome is risky. It wouldn't be considered faith otherwise. It would be a known calculation. Faith it until we make it, right? Choose love more. Where love is present, fear is absent. Love is from God and fear is not. *When we avoid what we are afraid of, it makes our fear even bigger.*

The more we grow in our experiences by embracing new things, the more confident we become. I have encountered people in my travels who have struggled with the idea of change. The comfort of staying in the safe zone can paralyze us from our ability to grow. It is okay to make poor choices. We need to pull up our bootstraps and move forward. We are not victim to our mistakes. Grow and Learn. Move and Grow. More faith and less fear.

When we move in faith, trusting the known will of God for our lives to make disciples and bring God glory by our ability to love on others in as many tangible ways as possible, we find peace that surpasses all understanding. Even in the thick of it where it's hard and messy, God uses us, and He fills in the cracks for what we are lacking. The good news is that we have everything we need right now. Don't even bother looking to the left or the right, as the thief of joy (comparison) will steal away our ability to see our own lane. Don't look back either, as that is not the direction of forward motion. **We can't be distracted by comparison when we are captivated by our purpose.**

Let me whisper some words of hope for you when I say we know the end of the story God wins. The more wins we have by saying yes to what matters, the more we win in living a life captivated by our purpose and plans God has for us: to not harm but rather to prosper, and to give a hope and a future. He or she who is brave is set free. Freedom comes in many forms.

Below are some questions to help you prioritize hope in your life

- What does a life of freedom look like for you?

- What are the dreams that God has planted seeds for in your heart?

- What can you do to cultivate a garden of love in your heart for God's purpose and plan for you?

- Write your answers down and bring them to life.

Speak out loud so that others can nurture and help you grow!

Traveling with Purpose

Truth be told, I am a total homebody. I love the space we call home. It's comfortable and safe. It's where my routine and my people are. It's my soft place to fall in the nook and cranny of my day. It comforts me daily. I bought a pillowcase a few weeks ago for our bed. It had a cute little dog on it, with the words *stay at home club*. When I go outside of my comfort zone away from home, I require the help from our Heavenly Father for peace, endurance, and a good ole fashioned kick in the pants to "do this." I have surprised myself, as the more impact I have had in my career, the more I have found myself traveling and being with other people, wherever they are. I like meeting people where they are at as that is their own safe place. This involves me moving out of my safe zone and meeting them in theirs. I find I can connect with them better when they are in their comfortable place. Even in my health coaching practice, I like to meet people in their home. It's where they feel safe and we can talk about things that matter to help them dial in some healthier habits.

Traveling outside my comfort zone to meet people is challenging for me, but that doesn't mean I can't do it. Just because we face obstacles doesn't mean we can't overcome them. We just can't do them on our own. And we aren't designed to. We are designed to be in community and fellowship with our Creator and seek Him for what we need to overcome. Maybe you love travel and it's where you get the most joy and find being still or home a challenge. There is no right or wrong in this. We are all uniquely woven for purpose and impact. The point is that we find out what makes us tick and use those beautiful intricacies for powerful moments our own lives and the lives of others.

On one of my most recent pleasure trips, I was getting ready in the hotel room and glanced down at the vanity where I was fixing my hair and makeup. I noticed a piece of hotel literature and a few of the words captured my eye. It said, *travel with purpose*. I thought to myself that we are all in our travels, whether we are at home or on the go, and we will always have purpose in the ordinary and in the extraordinary. I also realized in that moment that being called to disaster relief assistance means travel. And travel for me is going way outside of my comfort zone. How ironic that what I enjoy the least, is the mechanism that allows me to be used in such profound ways to help others in their time of need. *Isn't it interesting how God uses those things about us that we think would hold us back to have such incredible impact on others?* It is so comforting to me to know that God gives us what we need to do in order to live a life of impact, regardless of how we see ourselves and what we think we are, or are not, capable of doing.

For our household, travel means making arrangements for our fur babies. It means holding off on being able to coach a client in person. It means landscaping doesn't get maintained. There will always be things that will go by the wayside when we step out of our comfort zones to impact the lives of others. Those details are already worked out and smoothed over so that we can go and do what we need to do. We often hold opportunities at arm's length because we have predetermined it will be too difficult to pull it together. How arrogant it is for us to decide why, who, when, and what those things are? When did we forget that we aren't the Creator of the world?

Chapter 16: Happy Endings

Are happy endings even possible these days? Do you ever see tragedy and wonder how in the world are these people handling this with such grace and mercy? Do you ever look and ask yourself why can't these people see that it's possible for good to come from evil? I see so much in my news feed where people's lives take unexpected twists and turns. We get caught off guard by life happening and it's interesting to see how we handle these challenges in our humanity. I don't think we expect the things to happen to us that do. No one hopes that illness, car accident, job loss, children being sick, or heaven forbid—school shootings—will happen? This is the world we live in. I think because we expect things to always go smoothly and they often don't, we are blindsided and set back by these instances in a way that paralyzes us to be ineffective in what matters. Life doesn't happen to us, it happens through us. We have choices in how we respond to these situations and we see them how we want to see them.

To give an example, we mentioned that we recently went to our happy place, Disneyland. Disneyland has always had sad and grumpy people in it. It's always busy. It's often overcrowded and sometimes when it's super-busy, we question why we came. It's all how we see it. We had our patio door open to our hotel room, overlooking downtown Disney. They had construction going on, jackhammers galore. Eric got up and shut the door and said the construction noise was annoying. I didn't see it the way he was seeing it. I heard the sound of people who were headed to have fun. I heard music that is soothing to my soul. I heard what I wanted to hear. I saw what I wanted to see. The same goes for how we choose to live each day on this side of eternity. It's all how we see things and what we claim them to be in our mindset. If you choose to hear what is loud and annoying, that is what you will hear. If you choose to hear the music, then that is what you will hear. While sad things do happen in life that doesn't mean these sad things have to send us into the fetal position of choosing unhappiness.

There are so many people out there choosing to overcome life's adversities and see these as set ups for others' blessings. Those are our people. Those are the people I want to be surrounded by. Yes, they are going through adversity, and yes, we will go through adversity too. It's all what we do with it that makes all the difference. One day we will be held accountable for how we lived and **who we chose to be**. We will be accountable for the impact we did or didn't have. I don't know about you, but I choose to have as much impact as possible. That means living a life choosing to see the adversity we face as an opportunity for purpose and impact on others' lives. When we take the focus off ourselves and put it into purpose for others, we find that our perspective becomes loaded with massive purpose and impact for what truly matters in life. I don't want to miss the point and I don't want you to miss it either. The sooner we all figure this out and start living this way, the sooner we begin to see the point to it all. Choose to be happy in the beginning. Choose to be happy in the middle. Choose to be happy in the end. *It's who we choose to be that matters most!*

I often wonder what it would be like to go through life from point A (birth) to point Z (death), and not have experienced certain things. I often ponder what I would do if I was given a short time frame to live. A few weeks ago, I woke up having had a terrible dream that I was given 6 months to live. In the dream, the doctor said that the first three months would be life as I already knew it and the last three would be progressively moving towards death and the quality of my life would diminish. He said to do what I had always wanted to do in the next 3 months. I woke up sobbing.

I remember laying on my back and tears were streaming from my eyes like a faucet. Despite frantic efforts to turn that faucet off, the handle kept turning and turning *on!* I eventually got up, even though it was earlier than normal, just so I could focus on something different.

Dreams

My dreams are often so vivid that I wake up the next day and ponder the experience like it actually happened, when clearly it had not. I have had dreams where I look at Eric with a frown frustrated by how he behaved in my dream, and he's like, "Hey, you know that was a dream, right?" I also have this weird thing where when I climb in bed for the night and close my eyes, I immediately have this highlight-sort-of-flashback reel of my previous night's dream. I will leave this right here for someone to psychoanalyze and tell me what this really means.

There is this idea that there are things that we think about that we would want to do, see or experience to make our lives feel more complete. I can think of a dozen things right off the top of my head that I would want to see or do, and I am sure you can too. There are certain things that resonate with us, be it bucket list trips, or opportunities that we would want to experience before we say goodbye to this side of eternity. I have always wanted to vacation on those huts on the water in Bora Bora. I have always wanted to walk the cobblestone streets of England. I can also see myself doing missionary work in third world countries.

What are those things for you? Why do you suppose they matter? What I have found is that I have been afforded the opportunity to do things and see things I would have never expected to. Most I look back on pale in comparison to those that God has put in my heart to do. We think we want to see and do certain things, yet we still feel a void in our soul it didn't fill in the way we thought it would. I know that the memories we create in some of life's experiences are things that can impact and change the trajectory of people's lives for good.

I think about my kids and the things I have told them are important in life. Be a good person. Pay your bills. Get a good job so you can take care of your family. Find a place to serve at church. Always treat women well. Give back a percentage of your income to God. These are some basic things I would like to see them do. But there are things that we say and there are things that we do. What we show people speaks volumes over what we tell them. This concept goes back to the old adage: *do as I say, not as I do.* We want our words to match our lifestyle. It's like telling your kids don't be a liar and then you write a note to their teacher saying they were sick when you were really on vacation. I am starting to believe this is more and more important with each passing day. While I think I did an okay job raising my boys by good example in word and deed, I wish I had learned more of showing them about the living a lifestyle that matters in more profound ways early on. What will your life evidence be based on your belief? What will people say mattered most to you?

Identifying What Matters

We have always demonstrated the importance of prayer time with God, serving others and having a place to serve within the church. But part of me wants to sit my boys down and say, *You know these things we did that we thought were important? There are other things we could have done that mattered more.* I don't live a life of regret. I can only be accountable for what I truly understood something to be at the time. I do, however, have a better grasp on what kinds of things we can say or do that matter more. I want to be able to show others what those things are and document them in a way that empowers others to do more of what matters too.

When we have set out to help people impacted by disaster, I share what we are doing on social media, but not for some sort of accolade. I share these experiences to show people what it looks like to live out a life that matters. Dag Hammarskjold said that "Never for the sake of peace and quiet deny your own experience or convictions." If people see it differently, that is on their heart. I can't control how people perceive me. And as Dr. Wayne Dyer said, "What other people think of me is none of my business." I can only be concerned with pleasing God and doing what He places in my heart to do. I have also shared on live video what it's like while we are serving in disaster relief. I want our friends and family to see that it's a matter of first saying yes and then taking action. The more we say yes to what matters, the more courage it gives us to keep saying yes. Choosing to be brave gives us more courage. The more we do it, the more courageous we get. We need more of that in our society. Can you EVEN imagine what it would look like if we ALL took action?

Facebook has a 'go live' feature in our news-feeds, that allows us to publish a live video for the world to see what's happening while it happens. I wish Facebook and Instagram were around earlier as I would have wanted our children's grandparents to be able to see more of our kids' lives as they grew up. It would have given them the ability to watch more soccer games and school musicals. But that wasn't the reality of our time, a mere twenty years ago. Social media is such a unique animal. We get to document human behavior with total freedom of speech. It gives introverts the ability to say and do more than they would in person. I know this all too well, as I have a strong tendency towards introversion. What I value about this platform is that I get to offer out content that I might not otherwise say or do in person. It has given me more confidence in my belly-to-belly relationships. I have grown a lot personally in the past five years, especially since my health has had such a dramatic turn around.

I remember when I first went live on Facebook. It was a Friday morning, and I hadn't showered yet or even brushed my teeth. I had bed-head and was still in my pajamas. I honestly couldn't tell you a lot about that video except I was cooking breakfast and felt like I had something to share that morning that compelled me to say and do things I might not otherwise have said or done in person.

There is this invisible force field of confidence that social media platforms offer us. We can say and do things without a lot of consequence. We can even delete things that are said or captured live, and I thank God for that technology too! When the live platform first came out, I used it periodically in Facebook groups to help share information to people about their optimal wellness journey. At first, it gave us the option to decide who our audience was. It could be just you and then if you liked it, you could share it after the fact. If you didn't like it, you could immediately delete and not share.

There is something about 'going live in life:' to not have it be retractable. To totally put yourself out there in an authentic way, says, *I have a message to share and I'm not responsible for how you receive.* It's completely exhilarating while simultaneously making me feel like I want to throw up. It's quite a mix of emotions.

The point is that we all have something unique we want to share with the world. It's the way God made us. We all have things we are passionate about. Some of them are because we have had experiences we want others to be cautious of, and some we want to share because we want others to have that same great experience.

These are the God-given desires of our hearts. They are by design and they were planted even before we were woven.

Life as Intended

Would it be crazy to design something with a purpose and never get the experience to see it unfold? That is the longing of God's heart for our lives. He created us for His purpose and for His unique plan. We often skate through life missing critical junctures where He wants to see those things unfold. The more we stop to think what those things are and what it is we are created to do, the more this side of eternity will make sense. Don't we just want some more clarity to it all? Wouldn't it be a tragedy to go through life with this beautifully wrapped gift in our arms and never unwrap it? The braver we become 'going live' in our lives, the more others are able to see greatness in their own. Each of us are designed to unwrap that gift, and when we unwrap it, it gives others the ability to see it being unwrapped. I love the idea that I might be the only person in my kids' lives who can show them that attaining their God-given dreams are possible.

What if that was the main role to shepherding our kids? What if they need to see us 'walking it out' to give them the boldness to 'walk it out,' too? It's a holy responsibility to show others that what God puts in their hearts, we are boldly and confidently doing for them too. We hold space for others to step into their greatness. We step into our own greatness in order for others to step into theirs. Can you imagine if our entire society was believing greatness and living the lives God created them to? The more we are doing this, the bigger the ripple becomes. If you want to see a change in the way something is done, be the person to start making that change.

One small step into greatness turns into bigger steps of boldness, bravery, and confidence. Think of how we train for a marathon.

We start by putting one foot in front of the other, with a walk that eventually paces into a run. What is it you are feeling called to do? What will the impression of your footprint hold for others? Will you choose to see life's challenges as life's set ups for higher callings? Will you choose to see more extraordinary in the ordinary?

Let's go to a Movie

Who doesn't love a good movie? I love going to the movies. It's fun to go to a place where the world shuts off and we go into an alternate reality for a couple of hours. I think we do this with television too. We give ourselves permission to turn off all other forces around us and we submerse ourselves into an alternate reality. Some movies and TV shows allow us to feel better about ourselves, as we witness a false reality in which people navigate sometimes often very unrealistic challenges. We are taken into both the future and the past. We get to see and experience the life of others in a unique way.

Movies that are based upon true stories have an even more compelling impact on us. We connect with the story because it's something that happened to another human being. It validates our humanity, showing us we are not so alone in this world. Why, in a world filled with millions of people around us, do we feel so isolated? Are we not connecting with people in ways that matter? Is it safer for us to not connect, so that people don't see how we truly feel, and see life in a way that is actually happening? My favorite movies are from an era where life was simple. I connect with reality TV shows demonstrating how to decorate homes in a vintage, or farmhouse style as the most popular way to live and decorate.

I truly believe our society wants to be back in an era when life was simpler, but with all the comforts of quick delivery to our home or our inbox, rather than by horse drawn carriage and snail-mail. I remember going to the movies with Eric about a year and a half ago to watch a romantic comedy. When we left the theater, I was talking about how it filled my soul to turn off my phone, eat popcorn, and submerge myself into someone else's reality. As soon as I was able to purchase that movie so I could watch it anytime I wanted to, I did. I have watched it when I am cooking, cleaning, or just sitting and doing nothing. I can choose to have this experience where I am taken to a different place other than where I am.

Is that really our world? Do we really have it that bad? Is our current perception of reality so bad that we want to visit another version? It makes me sad to think of all the different ways we can alter our reality in order to numb our emotions and forget our experiences. I have a LOT to be grateful for. Sometimes I feel guilty for what I have, as I know there are so many people in this world who don't have what I do, get to experience what I have, or live life in comfort like I do. In reality, what we have is temporary. We often take it for granted.

We all have a level of capacity to which we have earned or been given, and there is a purpose in that capacity for each of us. We aren't given these things to hold on to tightly. They are allowed in our lives for us to use them to benefit others. When I seek people out to be there for them when disaster strikes, I use the time and financial resources God gives me. When there is a hole in ministry at church that we can physically fill because we have the time to do it, we better say yes. And the truth is, there is always someone who can watch your life like a movie, and see a 'false reality.' They covet the privilege you have, too.

Chapter 17: Expectation, The Thief of Contentment

Have you ever gone through a life experience and thought to yourself that you never saw it going that way? I know we all have. They say that comparison is the thief of joy. I think **expectation is the thief of contentment**. Especially living in North America, we have certain expectations of what we are entitled to in our 'free' country. The Bible says we are to consider it joy when we have trouble, and that we aren't promised a 'good life.' We are promised to have a God who is there for us always, who loves us unconditionally and promises to see us through. One who will never give us more than we can handle and will help sustain us.

I love inclement weather. Even though it's not always a great experience for everyone, I like choosing to see it as what we need. I like the idea of having to stay inside and not go anywhere, when we know a storm is coming and we might not be safe on the roads for a few days. I love going to the store to prepare and get stocked up on all kinds of comfort foods to cook and eat. Call me crazy but I like the idea that we are forced to stay inside and be together. I don't like being cold, but I do love the beautiful snow we get as a result of the drop in temperature and a decent storm. I also love snowshoeing. What a joyful experience for us to hike in the beautiful landscape of God's creation. Deciding to snowshoe means I know it will be cold, so I bundle up.

Living where we do, not only do we have four seasons, we get each season. Some years, they blur and blend together and some years we go from one drastic temperature to another. We have a saying here: if you don't like the weather, wait a minute because it will change. While I know there are extremes to weather that leave many people devastated, I appreciate how devastation and tragedy unite our society for a common cause. We meld and mesh without conjecture to the tone of our flesh or the inclination to our accent. It makes me wonder how much we could embrace as 'good and positive' instances like tragedy or disaster when it creates unspoken unity in communities. I have seen this first-hand, as I toil tirelessly to help people in time of disaster and tragedy, when working with our local community in various initiatives, and on a larger scale, with our efforts towards disaster relief.

I don't know why I value the inclement weather as I do. Perhaps it's the nature of our need for God and our true understanding that we don't have the control we think we have. It is humbling. He tells the sun when to rise and gives the wind its breath. We are meant to be there for one another. If we are given much, we should expect to give much. We aren't meant to have walls or boundaries to our humanity. We all put our pants on one leg at a time and one foot on the ground at a time. Just because the label is different, doesn't mean we are *that* different. We all navigate challenges and setbacks. The more people we have seeing that the setbacks are setups for each of us to step out into the God-given platform for greatness, the more people we have walking in unity with their God-given purpose. We are by design. We are for purpose.

With Purpose, for Purpose, on Purpose

We are each here to demonstrate how amazing our Creator is and how much He desires to be in our lives. I once had a friend tell me that he didn't see his need for God in his life was good by many standards. He had a great job, good health, a lovely wife, kids, and a nice home. I can understand how he would see it that way. And if you haven't ever experienced challenge or struggle, I could see where it might not occur to someone for a need for a Higher Power in life. But I can tell you with a resounding confidence that if you haven't been through a storm yet, you will, and God will see you through it. Once you are through, there will be a reprieve, to prepare for the next peak before you will hit the valley again.

The valley is where you can choose to learn and grow and ask God what He wants you to do with this valley rather than why He allowed the valley. It's not our job to know why things happen. It's our role to assume that He can use us in that valley for His glory and for His Kingdom. He will see us through it all! Ask Him to see you through. He created you with purpose, for purpose, and ON purpose. He wants to hear from you. He desires to be in relationship with you.

This will all make so much more sense when we truly grasp this understanding of the purpose that generates in the valley. Enjoy the peaks, reprieves, and times of rest and get ready for the next! It's all good. It's all how we speak about it and call it what it is. Call it a burden and it will be a burden. Choose to see it as a blessing, and a blessing it will be. It's all our choice to see and claim. Be patient with the process and know that if you are still in it, there is a good reason for it. He is God and we are not. We are not the main character in the story. I know we want to see and believe that we are, but ultimately, this life isn't about us. The sooner we rest in that peace, the sooner we can operate and live our lives as they are supposed to be lived. I value knowing there is a point to it all. So many people fail to see it and they are missing out on what it truly means to live a life surrendered to the One who made us.

Captivated by Purpose

When I was growing up, I didn't think we had money. The standard to which I based that on was by seeing what others around me had. I knew that my mom lived on a budget and that the answer to doing things and having things wasn't always yes. But when I look back on my life and think about the things we did when I was growing up, I still got to do what most kids got to do. I had swim lessons, mostly hand-me-down clothes, played soccer, and was a girl scout. I went to church camp and was able to be a part of the ski club that went to a high-end ski resort every Saturday during the winter season. We had Christmas every year, and I had a birthday with presents. How I measured what I had was based on what I could see others had and what they were experiencing around me.

By comparison, I didn't have all I wanted, but I had enough. I graduated high school when I was 17 years old and moved to a bigger city all by myself. I got a job, a place to live, and paid all my own bills. Somehow in the midst of not having what I thought I needed, I always had enough. My parents raised me to have manners and be respectful of others. Money doesn't buy those sorts of things. They read me the Bible and showed me a life that Jesus lived. I didn't understand what that foundation meant until I was old enough to process it as an adult and see it for what it truly was.

I think we live our lives the same way. We often wish we had more by comparison to what we saw some other people doing, when in reality, we always had enough. In fact, you have everything you need right here today to live a life that matters. It's a decision you make to see it the way that is worthy. Once you acknowledge what that life looks like, you will see the pieces of the puzzle as they are deemed to fit in perfect place and perfect timing.

You have the ability to have the kind of impact God created you to have. I can't have your impact. I also can't have the impact I put out there without you having yours. We are all designed to work together in each of our gifts, talents, and God-given dreams. My dreams are magnified when you are living yours. Can you even imagine what this looks like? It's a beautiful tapestry waiting to be woven! Please say yes. Keep saying yes, no matter if it's easy or hard. We can do hard things, you know. We do them every day and we just don't always acknowledge them. The more we each say yes, the more we are creating space for others to see us walk it out and they too can be inspired to walk out theirs!

Room for Cream

I have met a lot of people for coffee over the years. I remember my very first fancy coffee beverage at a local coffee chain. We had a friend of ours who had an espresso machine in his home, and he told us about the morning latte he makes himself and encouraged us that they were delicious. On his advice, Eric and I decided to try our hand at our first $4 latte. It was delightful! I loved everything about it from the time we walked in and the smell of coffee being brewed. I loved that we were by ourselves and didn't have any kids underfoot. It was a lovely experience. I have gone on to meet clients, friends, family, and even total strangers who became fast friends in coffee shops. In fact, I have always wanted to be a barista. Our son Garrett worked at a local coffee chain for three years before going into the military. It was his first job and as a perk he would sometimes bring us home fun drinks that were made in error or that were part of what he got being on the job that day. I remember his first and his last day like it was my own.

Truth be told, I would try and live vicariously through him since I had always thought it would be fun to work in a coffee shop. I love the idea of creating a unique experience for people to enjoy. Being at a coffee shop, whether I am by myself, with someone, or with a group of people and sipping on a cold beverage on a hot day or a warm beverage on a cold day, is a unique experience. When I ponder the price we pay for this experience, I know that most people in our society don't have this privilege I speak of.

As a health coach, it can be a bittersweet experience to share food and beverages with people, because I think about what it's doing to the inside of the body. Not everyone can tolerate the impact that caffeine has on the body even though there are antioxidant benefits. I know that non-caffeinated beverages are offered too. I see food and beverage differently than most. I consider it a blessing and a curse. I volunteer at our church in various capacities and recently I started volunteering at our church café where we have a full espresso coffee bar with Italian sodas and just about every coffee drink you can dream up. Currently as I share this, I haven't stepped up to be trained as a barista, but I know I will. The training is there for me when I say I am ready. I will know when the courage meter is high enough to do it and I will. In fact, my guess is that even by the time this book is published (God willing) I will have ventured out and gotten trained. But for now, I am a happy 'runner' in the café. I take the coffee order, put some syrup in and hand it to the barista for the milk and espresso magic to happen.

Not everything we can do on this side of eternity will make sense. Some people have gotten a good chuckle seeing me work the coffee bar at church, as they know that a lot of what is offered there would go against my lifestyle and my health coaching. I get it. But there was a need and I filled it. I think one day my longtime dream to be a barista will be fulfilled and it most likely will be in a place where people come to receive hope and an opportunity to learn and grow in understanding about living a life that matters. That is A-okay in my book! There is something about putting together a cup of coffee or tea for someone to enjoy and experience that makes my heart glad with joy. We don't always need to understand what we are doing or why and sometimes we just say yes to a need and maybe, just maybe, it will end up being more of a blessing to others than it is to us. And sometimes it's more of a blessing to us than it is to others when we say yes to the calling

God puts in our hearts. Why have I always wanted to be a barista? I have no idea. Why haven't I done it yet?

Most likely I have the expectation of making a mistake and I will let someone down. I will watch and learn and will get my comfort level up to overcome that expectation that I know is going to happen! It's okay to make mistakes. If there is ever a setting for someone to offer me forgiveness for that, I suppose church is that place!

For now, I am a happy runner and only God knows what tomorrow will bring! One small step turns into another bigger step towards each of our greatness. It may sound silly, but it matters a great deal to me! Sometimes we are called to leap it in faith and we are given the confidence we need to leap. Sometimes we take smaller steps and that is okay too. Small steps, medium steps, and BIG steps. What matters is we step it out one way or another. Don't be paralyzed by the fear of the unknown. Don't fill your cup so full that there is no room for God to add the cream; the good stuff. If God calls you to it, He will bring you through it, whether making fancy coffee or caring for orphans and widows. He equips the called.

Blurred Lines

I have had seasons in my life where everything is status quo. During these times there was not a whole lot happening one way or another. Status quo is a comfortable place to be in UNLESS you understand that you were made for more. I have acknowledged to people at times when I'm stepping out in faith with a new area of ministry or an opportunity for impact, that I know that opposition is going to hit the fan, and the struggle will be real for the foreseeable future. Because I know this all too well, I have avoided stepping out of my comfort zones at different times as I don't want to experience the challenge that typically comes when we step out in faith. The fact of the matter is, the Devil doesn't care if we sit at home on Sunday and watch football rather than take our family to church. He cares when we put our family in the car and make a choice to learn and grow in our faith. So, expect the struggle when you set out to choose a life of impact. When we are prepared for what is going to come, it won't catch us off guard. It's the barometer I use for knowing how bold and brave I am being, and how much I am stepping out in faith. We can acknowledge the struggle for what it is, embrace it, and choose to be victorious and not a victim. From where I come from, we are victors and all we do is win!

Clearly, we are living in compromised times in our society. We have morphed into a lot of ways that are very confusing for all of us since the beginning of time. I remember when I learned from my oldest boys some of their experiences they were having in high school were things I would have experienced in mature-audience rated movies when I grew up. I don't think our minds truly can ever form and mature to a place where we can make sense of where our society truly is. My husband receives notifications via news apps on his phone that recount shootings daily. What used to be isolated in bigger cities is now happening everywhere. No city is too small or off limits for the level of depravity to which we live. I believe we each have the ability to be an agent of change. I believe we have power and strength in numbers. I believe most people operate out of fear to stand up for what is right and not only advocate for themselves but to begin to have impact and advocate for others.

We have certainly lost our ways. Our attention is divided, and we have lost focus on what is important, valuable, and what is good. Our lines are blurred on what is good for the individual rather than the whole. More often than not, we have to let go of self more than we are inclined to do. We need to fight these inclinations like the plague.

Those inclinations are our sin nature. It's our nature to operate out of self. It's something for the greater good that we have to release so that we can become others focused. We are not designed or created to be an 'each man for himself' society. This is where depravity enters in a fierce and highly destructible way. It creates massive division and we lose site of what we are here for. We are here for community. We are created for that. It's why when we make a decision to be there for other people in the depths of pain, we find ourselves. *We find what we are created for, something that fills a space in our hearts we never even knew existed.* We wonder how did we ever function in life without having that anointed space. That my friends, is unique, profound, and holy.

I was taught once that choosing to sit in the front row is a powerful place. When we choose to sit in the front row, we choose to absorb things in a different manner. It says we are here, and we are eager and ready to learn. Sitting in the front row of your life is a choice. When I don't want to be watched, seen, or heard, I sit in the back. The back is complacent and mediocre. It's a safe seat to slip out quietly and no one will see.

Community is powerful for impact. When we choose to be part of a herd, it's harder to get 'picked off.' It's when we separate from our pack that we become vulnerable to walking away, as we have no true ties to what we are committed to doing.

We do this in our lives too. We sit at the back so that no one can see us in our frailty. We choose to be unwatched and unseen. Taking a position to stand up for others requires leadership. The more we walk in obedience, the more we find the amount of people following us in our obedience. When we choose the front row and to lead, it's inspiring for other people. We hold that space for them to be bold, brave, and confident to live out the plans God has for them when we do it first. We each have that ability to make that choice. We don't need special training or equipment. We are pre-wired for this kind of existence. We are pre-wired to lead, to have impact, and to be agents of change.

Our world needs change. We cannot keep going in the direction we are, and the reason we continue to go in that direction of depravity is because not enough people are walking in who they are created to be. I see that daily in my life, as I make choices to grow or not grow. The more I choose to grow, the more people I have following me. People follow people with a clear vision. Most people don't believe they have leadership skills. The choice we make to lead is inspiring. The more we do it, the better we get. The better we get, the more people we are leading. This is it, my friends. We get one shot. You may have thirty-five years on this side of eternity, or you may have sixty-five. We have to live our lives with the full knowledge that we are created for more and that what the world tells us that matters is deceptive, distracting, and void of true impact. Give yourself permission to be who YOU are created to be.

You are not a coincidence. You are part of a grand plan. Say no to mediocrity daily. When we become complacent and lack confidence in who God created us to be, the enemy wins. Complacency is a breeding ground for us to become victims. The more complacent we become, the more of a victim role we assume. Victims don't have success. We are victors, remember? How we respond to everything that happens to us is what happens through us. Nothing happens to you. Everything can happen for you and through you. You have to choose to not let things happen *to* you, but rather, through you. God gave us free will, which means we are given a choice. We choose every aspect of how we respond to life and how we choose to live our daily life.

Chapter 18: But First, Hope

Many people in our society seem to find more hope in their day by starting with 'but first, coffee.' I do enjoy a nice cup of coffee. Not so much for the need for caffeine, but I enjoy the morning experience of sitting with Eric and slowly starting our day reading, praying, and talking over a warm cup. There is something exciting about waking up to a ritual in our day that is encouraging and hope-filled. Hope is not something a lot of people have. We lose hope when we see things that our minds cannot process. We lose hope in our circumstances when our expectations are for something greater to happen. Greatness does happen when things seem uncertain, unexpected, and hopeless. What God allows into our lives creates a need for us to have hope for better. Hope for good to come from it. What else is there to rest on in difficult situations when we don't have hope?

In Nevada, we statistically have a lot of people who struggle with substance abuse and addiction. In most cases, people who turn to drugs and alcohol to fill parts of their souls to make sense of the world will lose hope. Two years ago, our church started an initiative in our county to secure homes for people who are struggling with addiction. It was to allow them to seek refuge, to find a place where they can begin the healing process of a life of sobriety. When we set up a refuge, we provide homes of hope for people who are without it. We are able to provide hope for people on a wide variety in their lives. We choose to seek it, in order to find it. The more we have dug into this initiative to provide places of hope, the smaller our world became. This initiative hit very close to home. We found that more and more of the families we were tightly knit with lacked hope. They were struggling with addiction themselves.

Once again, this opportunity for us to step out in faith and seek God to find our role in helping other people find hope, ended up filling a space in our hearts. It allowed a place for purpose, impact, and doing more of what matters on this side of eternity. Eric and I stepped out in faith to pray and seek what God would want us to do as our role in this initiative. The first logistical question was financing. We sought God for our role in that and He made it clear. The money God blessed us with over time became something that we could have released into our own lives for fun, for vacation, for nicer possessions, and a more comfortable retirement. Those things don't matter in the end. Money is not something that belongs to us. The job we have is what God provides. The talent to do that job is God-given.

We own nothing on this side of eternity and to spend the resources that God gives us on things that matter brings TRUE joy and meaning that transcends most understanding. When we travel and do things like disaster relief, we utilize the God-given resources to live those God-given dreams in our hearts. You were born with ideas and dreams that God designed specifically for you. Seek Him for how He desires you to live, so you can begin to fill the space in your heart that will bring you hope for tomorrow, and joy we rarely experience, but crave daily.

Most often we miss the mark on what we think that trinket, purchase, trip, or personal relationship will bring us. Ultimately those fail to fill the space in our hearts God gives us for the plans He has for us.

There are things in life that happen that we don't always understand why. We have all had them from varying degrees of loss, uncertainty, and stress. We can, however, trust the plan that our Creator has ordained our lives into existence down to knowing the numbers on our head. Hope breeds hope.

Why would I care about your ability to understand that you matter and what you do on this side of eternity matters? How does that help me if we are a self-seeking civilization?

If my purpose is to allow me to help you see you are not random, and what God put you here to do is orchestrated by Him, would that give me the satisfaction to stand before God to hear, "Well done, good and faithful servant"? Everything I have been through has created space for me to share the hope I have been given, to better understand why I was created, so that you can piece together why you were created.

Do you see where we are going with this? When you come to a place where you give thought to what God has planned for you and seek His direction on what He desires we do on a daily basis, we generate hope not only for ourselves but for others as well. Part of what you do has purpose for others. Decide to love yourself and what God created through you in your uniqueness so much, that His love seeps through your pores and drips onto others to give them clarity on who they have been created to be and to do!

I have addictive tendencies. I know this about myself. Because of this knowledge, I have set some boundaries up in my life to not broach areas that could cause me to stumble into hard-to-recover circumstances. I have never been one to consume alcohol, but I could see how I could become addicted to it. The reason I know this is because I do things in addictive mannerisms.

For instance, when I purchase a song that I like, I don't just add it to my playlist and listen to it here and there; I listen to it back to back, over and over. When I find passion in something, I pursue it hard. We can go to certain places in our minds with different things and we can really embrace them in ways that can be unhealthy not only for us, but others around us. Once we entertain and give thought to unhealthy things, it opens the door for it to have a foothold in our life. It can become something hard to recover from.

I think knowing this about myself has given me a certain level of compassion for others with destructive tendencies.

I know I could struggle with drugs or alcohol because of those tendencies to be addictive about certain harmless things, and therefore I choose to not have those things be something I even entertain. Because of this tendency, I believe I have compassion and a true desire to help those around me to be able to easily seek refuge from their addiction and pursue a higher level of hope. *We are all able to hold space for others in their healing process, and we all have the ability to generate hope by helping others rise from the ashes when the smoke clears or the waters recede.*

Believe that about yourself. Believe that you can help others rise above their ashes when they are in the thick of it. Take them by the hand and offer them hope by what God has done for you. Let them know you KNOW how they feel and what you found hope in. That space is sacred and exists solely for you to pass on to someone else.

It's not my Fault

We can only be held accountable for what we know. What I have learned is that our society doesn't value being held accountable for much. We want to do what we do and not have anyone or anything to answer to. When we do find ourselves in a place where we have erred, we have a reason why, and we have something or someone to blame. When we moved into our current home two years ago to be closer to our oldest son and his wife in their new home, we had an opportunity to paint our front door a different color than the previous owner had. We had the house painted when we first moved in and we needed to match the front door to the new color we chose for the home. We settled in on a gray color.

What we chose was hysterical because of what the name meant for us. The gray is called *it's not my fault*. That phrase is something we heard rather frequently raising three kids. Let's face it, as adults we too often find good reason for our misgivings, shortcomings, and the errors of our ways. Let's say you are holding a cup of coffee when someone comes along and bumps into you and shakes your arm making you spill your coffee everywhere. Why did you spill the coffee? "Because someone bumped into me, of course". Wrong answer. You spilled the coffee because there was coffee in your cup. Had there been tea in the cup, you would have spilled tea. Whatever is inside the cup, is what will spill out. Therefore, when life comes along and shakes you (which will happen), whatever is inside of you will come out. It's easy to fake it until you get rattled.

So, we have to ask ourselves the question, "What's in my cup?" When life gets tough, what spills over? Joy, gratefulness, peace, and humility? Or anger, bitterness, harsh words and reactions? **We choose** 100 percent!

Private Label

I would be remiss if I communicated to you a message that when God gives us desires to do things that matter on this side of eternity, it will be easy and without challenge. I already shared with you that I had a friend tell me once that he hadn't seen a need for God as his life was pretty good and he didn't have a whole lot to complain about or had any significant conflict that solicited a need to be saved. All I could think of, as these words were coming from his mouth was 'Just wait. It's coming.' And it does. God desires to be in a relationship with us. It's why He created us. He also has plans for our lives; plans He uniquely crafted each of us to do what He wants us to do. We are our own private label. He gave my friend, just like He gave you, a label that reads things that will bless your socks off. Mine is reading Carrie; wife, mother, sister, aunt, daughter, cousin, mentor, friend, holistic health coach, prayer warrior, disaster relief advocate…author? Who knew?

How does your label read? How will you brand yourself and your life in a way that others can come to peace in their uncertainty because you live your life in ways that may be uncomfortable sometimes? Could you choose to do it in a way that God shows up in mighty and powerful ways? He is there to carry you, so that you can minister to others time of need with empathy and with peace that surpasses all understanding.

Last night at dinner we were having a conversation about a situation with my son's new English teacher. There had been some overcrowding at his school, and they received some additional funds for allocation of new teachers. The school was transitioning his current class with this new teacher a quarter into his senior year. He was initially very frustrated by this new teacher coming in, because he had established a rapport with his existing teacher, having had her the previous year.

He liked her and was comfortable with her. She had encouraged him previously, giving him confidence. He wanted to be a better student because of her. They were given a project and the incoming teacher was talking to him and his partner about what they thought their project would be on. After sharing what their plans were and feeling confident in their decision, this new teacher barraged him with a series of questions that made him uncomfortable, demeaning their topic choice. He felt belittled and immediately wanted out. He sent me a text about how horrible his experience was with her and I gave him permission to change his schedule and find a way to keep his current teacher.

After giving it a little thought and prayer, God showed my son that it's not always about being comfortable, and that He would give him what he needed to stay in this class and navigate this difficult challenge ahead. Is it conceivable that he would be given the strength to get through this class with a difficult teacher and come out on the other side having persevered through this uncomfortable time in his life?

When we stop and realize that it's not always about us. Sometimes we are in people's lives who are broken, hurting, and need Jesus. We are called to be light in a dark world and God gives us what we need to accomplish the uncomfortable. It does not mean it will be easy. It means He gives us what we need to get through it. To whom much is given, much is expected. God expects great things from each of us. He expects us to be able to weather difficult times, difficult people, and difficult circumstances.

He promises to be there for us, to see us through, as we learn what it means to live a life worth fighting, a life that matters. Hurt people, hurt other people. While we don't know how hurt this teacher is, what if God teaches us perseverance and patience as we navigate living a life that matters with purpose, for purpose, on purpose even when we are uncomfortable and have hurt people we encounter in our lives.

Have you ever had a circumstance play out, afterwards you acknowledge that you didn't see it going that way? Or that it turned out better than you expected? Or not? God has the best intentions with our life. It's the very reason He created you to be so uniquely you, and me so uniquely me. I can't be you and you can't be me. His plans are to prosper, not to harm, and to give us hope and a future. Without hope, we struggle with what potentially lies ahead, with the expectations that good things are to come, as intended. Even the ones we didn't foresee playing out as we planned, but more along the lines of what God had planned for us. God is all-knowing. Wouldn't you want to know the God who knows all? To know Him is to love Him. To love Him is to be grateful for what He has done. When we are grateful for what He has done, we live our lives in a manner in which is was intended. It is conceivable that we could be so grateful for our opportunity for eternal life that we want other people to grab onto it as well.

This is what it looks like to live a life with intention. We embrace the fact that we were intended with purpose, for purpose, and on purpose, so that others can have the same opportunity we have been given: that free gift of eternal life. Joseph was a great example of what man had intended for evil, God used for the good. Our lives are intentionally made by the Creator of the universe, with unique plans for our lives to unfold in miraculous ways. When we choose to see it as God sees it, with incredible purpose—regardless of how we see it playing out—we can trust His plans and perfect ways. Sometimes we MacGyver our lives in ways that puts us in control and when we try to control and do things our way, we will find ourselves being unfulfilled and lacking true joy because we aren't experiencing our lives the way God intended. He intended us to live with peace, with hope, with purity, with compassion, with love, with steadfastness, with resolve and an immense amount of patience for others as they are still in the process of figuring out their true purpose. Life is still very confusing for them and when we operate out of confusion, we lack clarity.

Can you even begin to imagine what it would be like to create a human being with a plan and a purpose for that life, and have that person not see or operate their life as you had intended it to be lived? God has an incredible amount of patience with us in this pursuit of trying to figure it all out. He allows certain people in our lives that are challenging and difficult, so that we can grow and seek Him as our source of power to navigate those people and circumstances. He created us to KNOW Him and to be known. He created us to be loved and to love others. Are you allowing God to love you? He knows you, but do you KNOW Him? He intended to have a relationship with you and for you to come to a saving salvation of eternal life. While we are here on this side of eternity, there are things He has planned and intended for you to see, hear and do that are all apart of His great plan!

The "Not Yet" and the Nos in Life

There have been many circumstances in my life that I planned out, hoped for, and pursued that I never once sought God's counsel? We often make major life decisions based on what the world says are what we should have, see, do, and experience, never giving much thought to what the Creator wants. Have you ever prayed or hoped for something and God didn't answer the way you wanted? Sometimes his 'nos' and 'not yets' are the best for us. We aren't God, so wouldn't it be arrogant for us to think we know what is best for us? It's not up to us to know everything and why. This is where our faith and our trust in Him collide in how He intended our lives to be. Have you ever had a child ask you for something and you have to chuckle deep down inside, knowing there is just no way that the answer would be yes to their request for, good reason, but they would never understand why? God is our Father. We can't put conditions on God. We can't have conditions to our faith and trust. We have to be okay with every aspect of His plan for our life when we seek Him and His perfect will.

Chapter 19: The Great Distraction = The World We Live In

"Things which matter most must never be at the mercy of things which matter least." – Goethe

There is a life that the world says we should live and then there is the life that God intended us to live. We live in a world of mass destruction by distraction. We are told to be homeowners, have a great job we love, that pays us to live a life of amenities and comfort. We are to have X amount of kids and certain friends. We are to travel and have amazing experiences.

I will be the first to tell you I have pictured my life playing out a certain way according to the world's standards and have done things that I think will give me true satisfaction and enjoyment and walked away feeling completely empty. How is that possible? What we think matters by the world's standards is a very subtle yet deceptive way of taking us away from ourselves and our ability to walk out a life that God intended versus the way that the world says we should. If we aren't doing what we are called to do, the enemy wins. The huts on the water in Bora Bora are beautiful, but are they what God wants you to spend your time and resources on? Or perhaps he has blessed you with the financial resources to go and do something amazing like show up in other people's lives in times of their need.

We are all going to have those times of need. Someone else's obedience is tied to our blessing, and our obedience is tied to the blessing of others.

If we haven't made a choice for what we are living for, we are living life by default—acting out the scripts handed to us by family, friends, other people's agendas and the pressure of circumstances. This is not living as a person who knows the meaning and purpose of their life. It is, however, never too late to change focus. Love your life. Live your life.

Be content knowing God has incredible plans for you and you have a uniquely structured DNA to walk that blessing of a life out. He wants His best for your life. The minute you receive who God created you to be, you begin to choose to walk a life **as God intended it to be lived**.

I have seen God do some incredible work in my life in the eleventh hour. His timing and His ways ARE perfect. Sometimes it goes as we desire and sometimes it doesn't. We have to be okay with all of it.

There will always be things that will happen that will be out of our control and against our desires, but they will always be something God can use for us to grow closer to Him.

I read this morning that people who have been disappointed in their life by a circumstance playing out not as they would have liked, are inclined to reject the idea of God, as what God allowed in their life wasn't how they wanted it. I am here to tell you confidently that I am SO grateful that the things I wanted were not a part of God's plan for me. *His protection is just as beautiful as His provision*. When something doesn't go the way I think it should have gone, I thank God for the fact that He is the one who knows best for me. I am going to trust that as the reason of His plans and purpose for my life. What I had expected to be best was God's protection.

Sometimes life unfolds in ways that we could never imagine. I do find great joy in being able to help people in a variety of ways. I don't know that I will ever get used to the fact that my health was compromised for ten years, and how God gave me an opportunity to use that as a platform to become well and help other people set themselves free. I waited and hoped ten years for healing, and He provided it. There were times when I had stopped believing it was possible, as I had tried so many things and figured it might be one of the crosses to bear in my life. *God heal me. God heal me.* He was doing it all along. I just didn't know it yet. Not only did He heal me, He gave me a platform for the same satisfaction He got for providing me an opportunity to feel better. He gave me the ability to experience that same satisfaction He did. Just wow!

My body isn't perfect, and it won't be completely healed until I am in His presence one day. I am grateful for the process of progress and the opportunity to experience my life at a higher capacity just by feeling better. There was a negative balance in my health account and God was preparing me for abundance.

I am grateful that it stung so badly, so I could operate out of intense gratitude for the gift I have been given. What gift have you been given? What burden is being allowed in your life right now that you can change your focus, to see as an opportunity to grow closer to Him, and an opportunity to comfort others despite your challenges? We are never the main character in the story. It's not about us. It's always about God.

When I first started to write, I titled my manuscript, *When the Smoke Clears.* The freshest experience I had was to help people whose homes burned to the ground. The fire started by accident. Sometimes things happen by accident, and sometimes there are ill-willed, poor-intentioned people out there who do evil things. We are subject to it all in our broken world. Until everyone figures out who God created them to be, there will always be confused, broken people who make poor choices. Even when we know who we are in Christ, we still make poor choices. We sin intentionally and unintentionally.

There is always going to be a spark that could potentially start a fire in our life. Sometimes the wind comes up and stokes the fire. Sometimes the embers are a slow-burn, producing a ton of heat. Sometimes there is a raging fire happening and we feel the worst pain we can imagine.

With the varying degrees of fire that will be in our life, there will always be times when the smoke clears, and we come up for a breath of fresh air. In this reprieve we can ask a very powerful question: not *"Why, God, did you allow this?"* but *"What, God, can WE do with this? Clearly You are in charge and in control, and I trust You and Your plans for what is being allowed in our lives right now. How can we make You famous? How can other people come to know of the love, grace and mercy You want to extend to their lives? How can other people see me and my response to this allowed fire and know that something about me and my reaction to this circumstance has a Higher-Powered explanation and that the only explanation we can give is You, God?"*

There is beauty in every circumstance, because we are in it and God is in us. Our all-knowing, all-powerful God is in control and wants us to trust the process that our lives are living examples of how amazing He is. When we give Him permission to be in our lives, a beautiful tapestry of hope and purpose are being woven together for good.

God doesn't force Himself upon us. We have choices. We have free will. He wants to be in it with us, but we have to receive that gift for Him to be in control of our lives. He is in control, so we might as well turn it over to Him. It's a much more palatable process of our intended purpose to be lived when we acknowledge we need Him, and we trust His plans for it all.

Think Long, Think Wrong

Time is of the essence, my friends. We are not promised tomorrow, let alone the ability to finish out today. It's imperative we help you establish what matters for you, so you can live intentionally in the very near future. Married or unmarried. Single with the desire to be single. Single with the desire to be married. Don't wait.

This is not the part where we say, when XYZ comes into play, I will begin living the life of significance God desires for me. No matter what your status is, you can seek and carry out the plans God has laid out for you. The sooner you accept and believe this, the sooner you will be living a life of impact igniting people's ability to have more blessing released in their lives because of your yes. It's not rocket science. **Relationships, words, deeds are all a commodity we can spend, and the bank is endlessly funded by God to the capacity that He wants to fund**. We keep showing up and He keeps footing the bill. *There is nothing like having an all-inclusive all-expense paid trip to your life of significance that matters.* If what you desire to do requires resources, ask God for that. If what you desire to do requires an allocation for time you currently do not see having, ask for it. If you know the 'what' but not the 'how,' ask Him and he will show you.

Do it as soon as humanly possible. Speak it out loud and write it down so that you can bring it life. God is the giver of every good and perfect gift. He is our provider for everything He desires us to be doing. What is fleeting will pass and what is valued will hold a space of hope for others, that their lives have meaning and impact too. Be generous and give wildly of your time. Pursue people with immense patience and trust God to fill in every gap of what you are missing to do what needs to be done. Treasure the process and enjoy the ride.

May the God of all hope and peace fill you up like He has for me. His words are true, and they are life. Read them to know them, for to know them is to love them. To love them is to live a life that matters and will play out through the lens of the One who made you. This lens has complete clarity and focus regarding what you are here for and is seeing grace and mercy for our failings and shortcomings. This very lens views hope in light of the grace and mercy given to us daily. This very expensive lens was paid for with a price of life—His life in exchange for ours. **As He sees it, the lens never needs adjusting as it's perfect in its origin and capacity.**

I feel led to share some practical steps and ways that you can begin to live a life of significance and reflects more of what God created and intended you to live with respect to the physical body and the spiritual shell that you house. I have found that one of the top roadblocks I encounter when working with people to help them unpack a life of significance is actually believing they are worthy of having impact. If you don't value the capacity to which you were created, how in the world can you release the impact you were created to have? There will be a significant shift in your perception of how you see yourself. It's not conceited to value yourself as you are created: it's the confidence in He who resides in you and the beauty that can and should unfold through you. We are all fearfully and wonderfully made.

I truly believe that this lack of knowledge and confidence is what poises a person to make poor decisions in life, where lack of good judgment and belief in who they are created to be sets the course for poor choices that escalate into what seems as an unrecoverable life. No matter where you are or what you have done, you are never too-far gone! This belief that we have in ourselves can catapult and create impact not only for our lives, but as hope for others.

We each have our own mark that we can have in our time here. What you can offer and be present for in your life very well could be quite different than what I can. That's the unique nature to your calling: that only YOU can facilitate for you and for others. That life of significance you are designed to have is not a secret or something God needs to contemplate. When you tap into it, the heavens will rejoice! God wins the lottery every day when we open our eyes to see who it is we are created to be.

When you begin to unfold the path laid out for you, the floodgates will open for others. There are people waiting for you to unleash who you are so that they can release and learn who they are as well. This is not the time to let fear hold you back. God has your back on this. He has brought you this far, so that you can show others that their mountains can be moved. It's time. Please do not let another day go by without progressively making small steps in the direction of putting pen to paper for what God has already scripted out for you. The great author of your life is waiting patiently for you to show up. But He is looking at His watch in anticipation and hopes that you don't dilly-dally another day longer to unleash the greatness He has planned for you. It's okay to have had things happen in your life that don't seem like they should be celebrated.

God brings us through those things. This is the *beauty we are to embrace that comes from the ashes.* It's okay for us to celebrate the challenges and setbacks that have unfolded in our lives as setups for other people to receive comfort and knowledge that someone just like them has been in their shoes. Validation is a key component for our humanity to receive comfort that we are not alone. We are not created to be alone or live in solidarity. There is something really special here I want you to understand. What you think you have experienced in life that has brought you joy is mostly likely not the true joy God designed for your life. There is this whole other space in your heart that is completely untapped and when you tap into it, the heavens will rejoice, and you will experience a peace and an ongoing passion like you could ever imagine. The only thing I can assure you, is to not trust what I say, but to trust the One who made you that His plans and His ways are THE BEST!

Chapter 20: Get Your Vessel Ready

Physically, it doesn't take much more than a 'yes' and a commitment to yourself to start stepping out in faith. Having walked out a lot of aspects of life of faith when battling illness was hard, but I did it. Knowing what the impact is like when the body is well is profoundly better. There are some simple things you can do to get your body in shape for the journey of having a life with more impact. What is important to know is that you don't have to have it all lined up before you say 'yes.' You simply need to work that vessel in a direction of a sounder structure to house the greatness you are created to be. You are so worth being set free!

1. Drink half your body weight in ounces of water per day. It's really that simple. Our bodies are 75% water. Give it what it needs, in order for you to feel your best.

2. Less alcohol and caffeine. Less does not mean none, but in case you are erring more on the side of an unhealthy consumption that may cloud your judgment less is better.

3. Limit foods with antibiotics and hormones. While we can't always control what foods we encounter out in public and when we travel, the more we control inside the home, the better. Mainstream meat, dairy, and poultry have antibiotics and hormones that disrupt our vessel from being the best it can be.

4. Less meat, dairy, and sugar. This doesn't mean none, just perhaps less than you are doing if you are overdoing it and you KNOW if this is a struggle for you.

5. Probiotics are a must. There are good, better, and best quality products out there. Not all probiotics can be absorbed by the

body. What is found at mainstream stores are not great. Get a good quality as it matters.

6. Get 7-8 hours of sleep at night. Rest is best for the vessel that will have impact.

7. Aim for at least one vegetable at each meal and start your meal by eating your veggies.

8. Strengthen your immune system with a good whole food multivitamin.

9. Less processed packaged foods. Anything packaged should have five or less ingredients and if you cannot pronounce the words, don't put it in your body.

10. Move your body. Find a form of exercise or activity that you can do at least 4 days a week. If you don't love it, you will make excuses not to do it.

11. We are all deficient in Omegas 3, 6, 9, 5, and 7. These protect our heart and brain and decrease our body's ability to let stress and anxiety impact us. Plant based is better, so you don't have to worry about the fish source.

12. Plant based supplementation will help keep balance to the amount of sugar regulating in your blood, so you are vibrant and vital.

Spiritually:

1. Find a church to belong to that preaches God's word, operates by His principles, is baptizing, and growing in members.

2. Get connected in that church with a place you can serve.

3. Find a smaller group of people in that community you can find fellowship with at least once a week to help hold you

accountable, where you are growing and doing things that matter while studying God's Word.

4. Pray daily about where God wants you to be, both bigger picture and in your daily life.

5. Read the book, *The Dream Giver*, by Bruce Wilkinson as soon as possible. Write out and speak aloud the God-given dreams He has planted in your heart. Go and do those things as much as possible.

6. Ask people around you what their dreams are and help them find their dreams too.

7. When you have challenges in life, which you will, find someone you can talk to, and share with them what it is that you are learning as you grow through it. Consider sharing with others, as God brings you through it what you could share with others who may be going through the same struggle. This is where you will find purpose in the struggle. Things happen through us and not to us!

I don't want people to see my life, things I have, and want those things. I want people to see the things I do and be inspired that they can do them too. I want them to feel compelled to think outside of themselves in that they are, by design, to operate with the time, talents, and dreams God puts in their hearts to do. I want more people seeing and doing the things that matter with what they have been given. It's not uncommon for me to see people like Bob Goff and say, "take me with you!" I want Bob to take me with him! I am not after the things he is saying he has. I am in pursuit of the type of things he is doing. I want people to see *your* life being lived out in a way that they say that about YOU! That is the kind of impact we should all be having. We don't want people coveting what we have.

We want people being inspired to do what we do! It needs to be simple and it needs to matter. People are watching **Who You Choose To Be**. If you are raising a family, those kids are watching you like a hawk and soaking in every word like a sponge as to how they should live their lives. You are a role model. God gave them to you not to race them from sporting event to sporting event, but to show them a life worthy of the manner in which God has called them to live. Those are forms of distractions that detract us from living a more purpose-filled life. I have been there, and done that, and knowing what I know now, I would definitely see it differently. We are to help them pursue the plans that God puts in their hearts, and show them that their God-given dreams are possible too! *Too many of us are chasing an "American dream" and that dream has so many people deceived into a false sense of what we are truly here to become.*

Chapter 21: Stop for Just One Minute

I know it's hard to do because we are so fast-paced as a society, but just stop for one minute and think about what it is you could be doing that matters. Do you really want to wait until the diagnosis that leads to the last three months of your life to do what you were created to do? Or do you want to live today like there is no tomorrow and like your time is borrowed? We are not promised tomorrow, and we are not promised this false reality we are shown on TV and in the movies. Life is messy and muddy. Pull up your bootstraps and prepare to get dirty. Don't worry about what you are going to track in the house, over what it is you are doing that gets you dirty. There is a whole eternity to 'clean and whole.' What will your highlight reel show others? Will it matter? Will you have chosen to make today a defining moment? To no longer live in complacency, but a life of purpose with more of what matters on this side of eternity?

I want you to think for a moment about your life as it has unfolded thus far. Think about the experiences you've had. Are there things you learned the hard way, things you wished you had done differently? Tell people. Are there ways you did something great and if you told people about it, it would help them do well too? Talk to others and share your story. Is there something you said to someone you wished you hadn't? Tell them that. Is there something you said to someone that helped them? Tell more people about that. Have you ever had something painful happen to you, found something you did helped you heal and move on? Tell more people. Have you ever had an idea for business or personal life that helped you do something in a way that it would help others if they did it the same way? Be bold. Be brave. Share your story!

There are no bad experiences in life. We can choose to learn from them and help others mitigate their future shortcomings, or we can choose to become a victim to those circumstances, which will impede our purpose to help others move their own mountain. Have you ever considered the fact that God moves mountains for you so that others can see them be moved? Yes, do more of that. We are a society that is captivated by narcissism. That is not who we are created to be. We are created to be self-LESS, which we need to be on purpose. In our sinful nature, that doesn't come easily. It comes when we choose to be selfless intentionally. It goes against the grain of our humanity. The more we choose to think of our self less, and think of others more, the more we begin to scratch the surface of **Who We Choose To Be** that matters!

About the Author

Carrie is a wife, mother, and a Board Certified Holistic Health Coach. Currently living in beautiful Northern Nevada with her husband, Eric, Carrie has raised 3 amazing young men, Jared, Garrett, and Caleb, who have given her tremendous joy and contentment through the gift of motherhood. She attended The Institute for Integrative Nutrition, the number one nutrition school in the world and is committed to working with people to become the best, healthiest, happiest, most purpose-filled version of themselves.

Carrie loves to spend time with her beloved family, coaching her health clients, going to bible study, and participating in church activities. She also finds great peace and purpose in living-out her God-given dream of offering hope to those who are working through the aftermath of natural disaster. Carrie and Eric work closely with the Samaritans Purse organization by traveling to those in need when needed.

"My clients are people working towards a better life, implementing both nutrition and supplemental changes to heal the root cause of theirs issues. They are running a long-term marathon towards their optimum health and lifestyle versus trying to sprint to a quick fix. In my practice, I blend health and faith to guide clients as they discover what it is that God has placed on their heart to impact this side of eternity. Our lives become so powerful when we choose steward our vessel well and learn how to use that better version of us for incredible impact that matters." - Carrie